Vanessa-Ann's
Holidays In Cross-Stitch

1 9 9 1

The Vanessa-Ann Collection Staff

Owners:
Terrece Beesley Woodruff and Jo Packham
Executive Editor:
Margaret Shields Marti
Editors:
Ana Ayala
Lisa Dayton
Tim Fairholm
Reva Smith-Petersen
Needlework Director:
Nancy Whitley
Graphic Artist:
Julie Truman
Graphing Director:
Susan Jorgensen
Operations Director:
Pamela Randall
Art Director:
Lynda Morrison
Administration Assistant:
Barbara Milburn
Controller:
Gloria Baur
Customer Relations:
Vicki Burke
Inventory Control:
Lisa Miles

Designers

Frank and Judy Bielec
Trice Boerens
Dale Bryner
Linda Durbano
Debbie Fair
Linda Hendrickson
Kristen Ford Kapp
Margaret Marti
Florence Stacey
Terrece Woodruff

Vanessa-Ann's
Holidays In Cross-Stitch
1991

Linda—
Remember mudpies, remember slides,
Remember swimming and places we'd hide.
Remember boyfriends and broken hearts,
Remember marrying and moving apart.
Remember the happiness, remember the tears,
The moments shared through all these years.
And that is why to you I'll send
This special message: I love you, friend.

Love,
Jo

Library of Congress Catalog Number: 86-62285
ISBN: 0-8487-0793-1
ISSN: 0890-8230
Manufactured in the United States of America
First Printing 1990

Executive Editor: Nancy Janice Fitzpatrick
Director of Manufacturing: Jerry Higdon
Associate Production Manager: Rick Litton
Art Director: Bob Nance
Copy Chief: Mary Jean Haddin

Holidays In Cross-Stitch 1991

Editors: Laurie Anne Pate, Kim Eidson Crane
Editorial Assistant: Shannon Leigh Sexton
Assistant Copy Editor: Susan Smith Cheatham
Production Assistant: Theresa L. Beste
Designer: Diana Smith Morrison
Computer Artist: Karen L. Tindall
Artist: Eleanor Cameron
Photographers: Ryne Hazen, Mikel Covey

The Vanessa-Ann Collection extends a very warm
thank-you to Mary Gaskill of Trends and
Traditions, Historic 25th Street, Ogden, Utah, for
letting us use her store for most of the
photography in this book.

To find out how you can order *Cooking Light*
magazine, write to *Cooking Light*®, P.O. Box
C-549, Birmingham, AL 35283

1 9 9 1
Contents

Introduction

Holidays, with all the anticipation and excitement that each one brings, are measures by which we gauge the passing of time. Each year is filled with special days, such as family birthdays, anniversaries, and various seasonal festivities. Coming each year, they make a cycle. This cycle of events is our personal record of time.

We at The Vanessa-Ann Collection hope that *Holidays In Cross-Stitch 1991* will help you record those events. We wish you hours of stitching pleasure and then years of enjoyment as you celebrate with the occasions remembered here.

1991

JANUARY
S	M	T	W	T	F	S
		1	2	3	4	5
6	7	8	9	10	11	12
13	14	15	16	17	18	19
20	21	22	23	24	25	26
27	28	29	30	31		

FEBRUARY
S	M	T	W	T	F	S
					1	2
3	4	5	6	7	8	9
10	11	12	13	14	15	16
17	18	19	20	21	22	23
24	25	26	27	28		

MARCH
S	M	T	W	T	F	S
					1	2
3	4	5	6	7	8	9
10	11	12	13	14	15	16
17	18	19	20	21	22	23
24	25	26	27	28	29	30
31						

APRIL
S	M	T	W	T	F	S
	1	2	3	4	5	6
7	8	9	10	11	12	13
14	15	16	17	18	19	20
21	22	23	24	25	26	27
28	29	30				

MAY
S	M	T	W	T	F	S
		1	2	3	4	
5	6	7	8	9	10	11
12	13	14	15	16	17	18
19	20	21	22	23	24	25
26	27	28	29	30	31	

JUNE
S	M	T	W	T	F	S
						1
2	3	4	5	6	7	8
9	10	11	12	13	14	15
16	17	18	19	20	21	22
23	24	25	26	27	28	29
30						

JULY
S	M	T	W	T	F	S
	1	2	3	4	5	6
7	8	9	10	11	12	13
14	15	16	17	18	19	20
21	22	23	24	25	26	27
28	29	30	31			

AUGUST
S	M	T	W	T	F	S
				1	2	3
4	5	6	7	8	9	10
11	12	13	14	15	16	17
18	19	20	21	22	23	24
25	26	27	28	29	30	31

SEPTEMBER
S	M	T	W	T	F	S
1	2	3	4	5	6	7
8	9	10	11	12	13	14
15	16	17	18	19	20	21
22	23	24	25	26	27	28
29	30					

OCTOBER
S	M	T	W	T	F	S
		1	2	3	4	5
6	7	8	9	10	11	12
13	14	15	16	17	18	19
20	21	22	23	24	25	26
27	28	29	30	31		

NOVEMBER
S	M	T	W	T	F	S
					1	2
3	4	5	6	7	8	9
10	11	12	13	14	15	16
17	18	19	20	21	22	23
24	25	26	27	28	29	30

DECEMBER
S	M	T	W	T	F	S
1	2	3	4	5	6	7
8	9	10	11	12	13	14
15	16	17	18	19	20	21
22	23	24	25	26	27	28
29	30	31				

JANUARY 1
New Year's Day

11:57, 11:58, 11:59. . . Start the music! The New Year is here, and this feline is fit as a fiddle, ready to "string" in 1991 on a happy note!

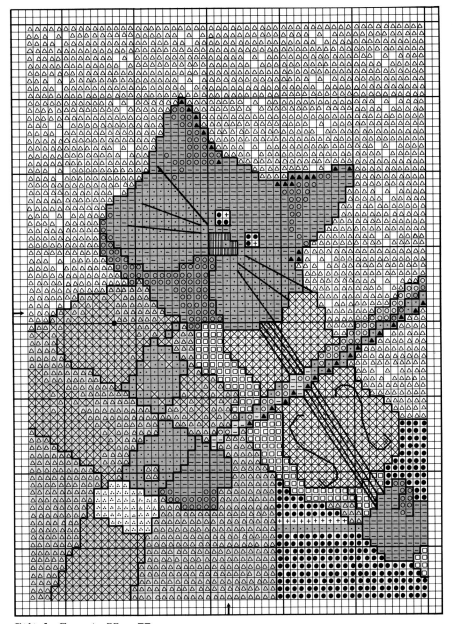

Stitch Count: 55 x 77

Tuxedo Cat

SAMPLE

Stitched on white Aida 14, finished design size is 3⅞" x 5½". Fabric was cut 10" x 12".

FABRICS	DESIGN SIZES
Aida 11	5" x 7"
Aida 18	3" x 4¼"
Hardanger 22	2½" x 3½"

Anchor		DMC	(used for sample)
Step 1:	Cross-stitch (2 strands)		
1	·		White
292	−	3078	Golden Yellow-vy. lt.
887	O	3046	Yellow Beige-med.
47	∴	843	Christmas Red (Marlitt)
43	△	815	Garnet-med.
266	+	3347	Yellow Green-med.
216	●	367	Pistachio Green-dk.
363	✕	436	Tan
309	□	435	Brown-vy. lt.
398	−	415	Pearl Gray
400	⊙	414	Steel Gray-dk.
401	▲	413	Pewter Gray-dk.
401	✕	846	Ash Gray-vy. lt. (Marlitt)
403	△	801	Black (Marlitt)

Step 2: Backstitch (1 strand)

403		310	Black

Step 3: Long Stitch (1 strand)

403		310	Black (whiskers, fiddle strings)

Step 4: Satin Stitch (1 strand)

403		801	Black (Marlitt)

Step 5: Silk Flower Placement

JANUARY 18
Hat Day

What's this? A holiday you've been missing? Well, hold on to your hats! These charming hatbands are a great way to get into the spirit of Hat Day.

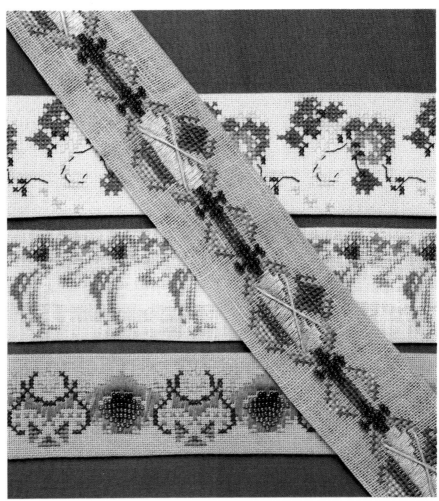

Fancy Hatbands

SAMPLE for Floral
Stitched on ivory Linda 27 over 2 threads, the finished design size is 2⅛" x 1½" for 1 motif. See instructions before cutting fabric.

FABRICS	DESIGN SIZES
Aida 11	2⅝" x 2½"
Aida 14	2⅛" x 1½"
Aida 18	1⅝" x 1½"
Hardanger 22	1⅜" x 1¼"

SAMPLE for Beaded Heart
Stitched on celery green Linda 27 over 2 threads, the finished design size is 2½" x 1⅜" for 1 motif. See instructions before cutting fabric. See Suppliers for Mill Hill Beads.

FABRICS	DESIGN SIZES
Aida 11	3⅛" x 1¾"
Aida 14	2⅜" x 1⅜"
Aida 18	1⅞" x 1"
Hardanger 22	1½" x ⅞"

SAMPLE for Sea Breeze
Stitched on white Belfast Linen 32 over 2 threads, the finished design size is 1¼" x 1¾" for 1 motif. See instructions before cutting fabric.

FABRICS	DESIGN SIZES
Aida 11	1⅞" x 2½"
Aida 14	1½" x 1⅞"
Aida 18	1⅛" x 1½"
Hardanger 22	1" x 1¼"

Floral

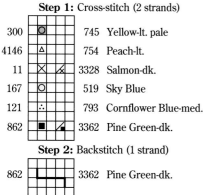

Anchor		DMC (used for sample)	
Step 1: Cross-stitch (2 strands)			
300	O	745	Yellow-lt. pale
4146	△	754	Peach-lt.
11	X	3328	Salmon-dk.
167	O	519	Sky Blue
121	∴	793	Cornflower Blue-med.
862	■	3362	Pine Green-dk.
Step 2: Backstitch (1 strand)			
862		3362	Pine Green-dk.

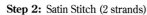

Beaded Heart

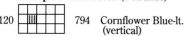

Anchor		DMC (used for sample)	
Step 1: Cross-stitch (2 strands)			
893	-	224	Shell Pink-lt.
970	△	315	Antique Mauve-vy. dk.
121	△	794	Cornflower Blue-lt.
940	∴	792	Cornflower Blue-dk.
Step 2: Satin Stitch (2 strands)			
120	▥	794	Cornflower Blue-lt. (vertical)
Step 3: Beadwork			
	+	00557	Gold
	●	00553	Old Rose
	□	00561	Ice Green
	X	00330	Copper

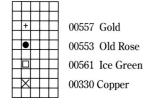

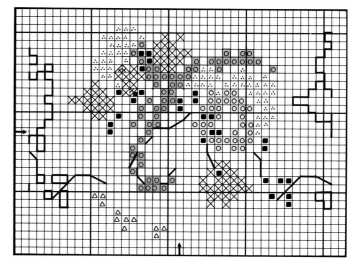

Stitch Count: 29 x 21 (1 motif) (Floral)

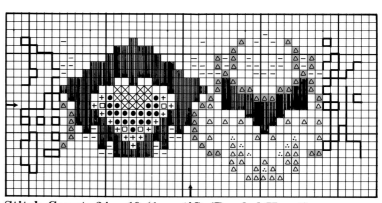

Stitch Count: 34 x 19 (1 motif) (Beaded Heart)

SAMPLE for Southwestern

Stitched on sand Dublin 25 over 2 threads, the finished design size is 3⅜″ x 1½″ for 1 motif. See instructions before cutting fabric. See Suppliers for Sterling Threads, Emotion Wild Braid, and Mill Hill Beads.

FABRICS	DESIGN SIZES
Aida 11	3⅞″ x 1⅝″
Aida 14	3″ x 1¼″
Aida 18	2⅜″ x 1″
Hardanger 22	1⅞″ x ⅞″

MATERIALS

Completed cross-stitch design
Matching thread

DIRECTIONS

All seam allowances are ¼″.

1. Before stitching design, measure around hat just above brim and add 2″ for horizontal measurement. Add 6″ to vertical measurement of motif. Cut unstitched fabric to match measurements.

2. Centering design vertically, begin stitching first motif 1″ from end of fabric. Repeat motif across fabric, leaving 1″ unstitched at opposite end. Heavy lines on graph indicate placement of additional motifs.

3. Measure 1½″ above and 1½″ below design and trim fabric. Trim ¾″ from each end.

4. With right sides facing and long edges aligned, fold design piece in half. Stitch long edge to make a tube. Turn right side out. Position seam in center back and press.

5. Wrap band around hat just above brim. Fold in seam allowance on 1 end of band. Insert raw edge of other end into folded end. Slipstitch ends together.

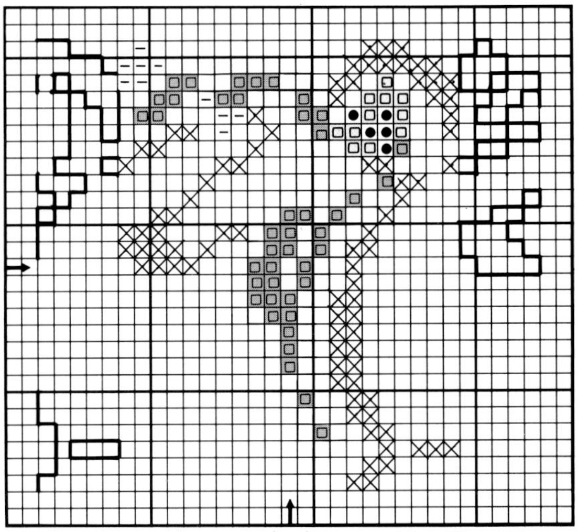

Stitch Count: 21 x 27 (1 motif) (Sea Breeze)

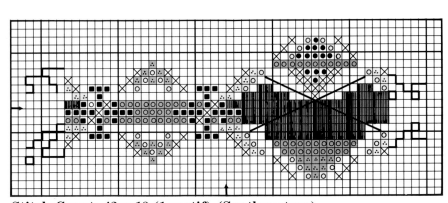

Stitch Count: 42 x 18 (1 motif) (Southwestern)

Sea Breeze

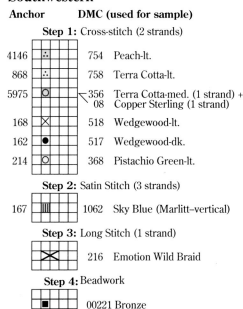

DMC		Marlitt (used for sample)
Step 1: Cross-stitch (2 strands)		
899	–	275 Rose-med. (Flower Thread; 1 strand)
335	▢	881 Rose
816	●	894 Garnet
519	✕	1062 Sky Blue
368	▨	418 Pistachio Green-lt. (Flower Thread; 1 strand)

Southwestern

Anchor		DMC (used for sample)
Step 1: Cross-stitch (2 strands)		
4146	∴	754 Peach-lt.
868	∴	758 Terra Cotta-lt.
5975	○	356 Terra Cotta-med. (1 strand) + 08 Copper Sterling (1 strand)
168	✕	518 Wedgewood-lt.
162	●	517 Wedgewood-dk.
214	○	368 Pistachio Green-lt.
Step 2: Satin Stitch (3 strands)		
167	▥	1062 Sky Blue (Marlitt–vertical)
Step 3: Long Stitch (1 strand)		
	✕	216 Emotion Wild Braid
Step 4: Beadwork		
	■	00221 Bronze

Welcome Spring

During the cold winter months, everyone longs for the fresh, sunny days that springtime brings. The folks at Longwood Gardens, in Kennett, Pennsylvania, begin their thoughts of spring even in the midst of snow. At Longwood Gardens, spring is welcomed in January amid the green lawns, palm trees, and flowers of the conservatory. You may not have a conservatory, but you can stitch this gull in flight, bringing warm tidings from tropical isles.

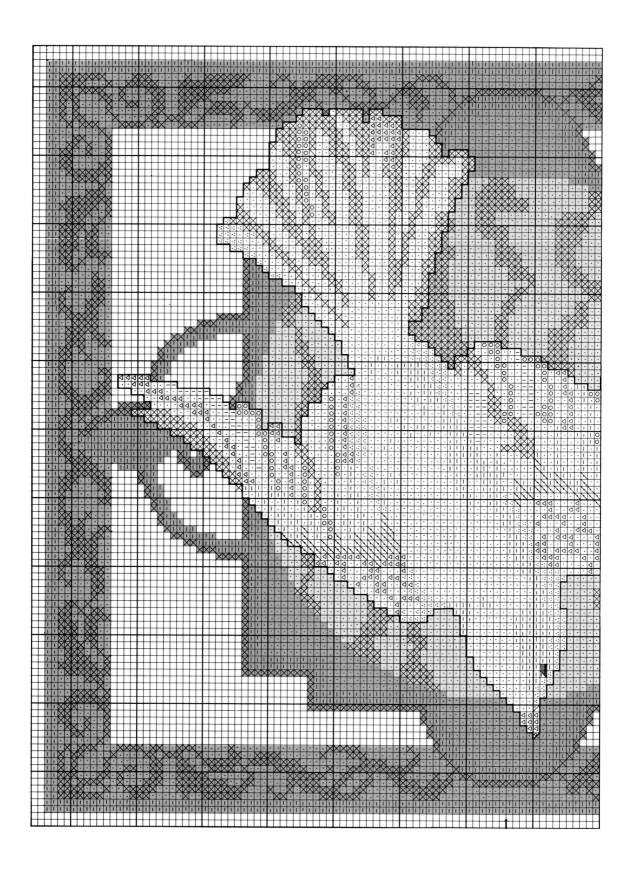

Stitch Count: 110 x 140

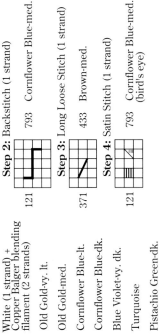

Anchor   **DMC (used for sample)**

Step 1: Cross-stitch (2 strands)

Anchor		DMC	
1	⋅		White
1	−	092	White (1 strand) + Star Pink Balger blending filament (2 strands)
1	✕	024	White (1 strand) + Fuchsia Balger blending filament (2 strands)
1	∴	023	White (1 strand) + Lilac Balger blending filament (2 strands)
1	◢	012	White (1 strand) + Purple Balger blending filament (2 strands)
1	○	014	White (1 strand) + Sky Blue Balger blending filament (2 strands)

1	△	021	White (1 strand) + Copper Balger blending filament (2 strands)
886	⧄	677	Old Gold-vy. lt.
890	⊡	729	Old Gold-med.
120	−	794	Cornflower Blue-lt.
121	⋅	793	Cornflower Blue-dk.
119	✕	333	Blue Violet-vy. dk.
167	□	597	Turquoise
216	✕	367	Pistachio Green-dk.
878	●	501	Blue Green-dk.
942	⋅	738	Tan-vy. lt.
363	✕	436	Tan
397	−	762	Pearl Gray-vy. lt.

Springtime Flight

SAMPLE

Stitched on wedgewood Lugana 25 over 2 threads, the finished design size is 8¾" x 11¼". The fabric was cut 15" x 18".

FABRICS   **DESIGN SIZES**

Aida 11   10" x 12¾"
Aida 14   7⅞" x 10"
Aida 18   6⅛" x 7¾"
Hardanger 22   5" x 6⅜"

FEBRUARY 14
Valentine's Day

Love can be many things. Sometimes it's careless, many times it's playful, and other times it's shy. Let one of these mimes—or all three of them—deliver your message to that special Valentine. Or, you can stitch one of the Valentine Sentiments on a perforated-paper card and then inscribe it with your favorite love poem. Better yet, write your own verse. Whichever you choose, your labor of love will not soon be forgotten.

Mimes Trio

SAMPLES

Stitched on white Jobelan 28 over 2 threads, the finished design size is 4" x 4⅞" for Careless Love, 4⅝" x 6⅛" for Playful Love, and 3¼" x 4⅞" for Shy Love. The fabric was cut 10" x 11" for Careless Love, 11" x 13" for Playful Love, and 10" x 11" for Shy Love.

Careless Love

FABRICS — **DESIGN SIZES**
- Aida 11 — 5⅛" x 6¼"
- Aida 14 — 4" x 4⅞"
- Aida 18 — 3⅛" x 3⅞"
- Hardanger 22 — 2½" x 3⅛"

Playful Love

FABRICS — **DESIGN SIZES**
- Aida 11 — 5⅞" x 7¾"
- Aida 14 — 4⅝" x 6⅛"
- Aida 18 — 3⅝" x 4¾"
- Hardanger 22 — 3" x 3⅞"

Shy Love

FABRICS — **DESIGN SIZES**
- Aida 11 — 4⅛" x 6¼"
- Aida 14 — 3¼" x 4⅞"
- Aida 18 — 2½" x 3⅞"
- Hardanger 22 — 2⅛" x 3⅛"

Anchor		DMC (used for sample)
Step 1: Cross-stitch (2 strands)		
1	○	White
300	–	745 Yellow-lt. pale
306	■	725 Topaz
290	✕	973 Canary-bright
4146	+	754 Peach-lt.
868	⸭	758 Terra Cotta-lt.
9	◇	760 Salmon
46	◉	1017 Christmas Red-bright (Marlitt)
47	●	893 Christmas Red (Marlitt)
108	·	211 Lavender-lt.
105	□	209 Lavender-dk.
110	◪	208 Lavender-vy. dk.
851	⊠	924 Slate Green-vy. dk.
397	◨	762 Pearl Gray-vy. lt.
403	◄	310 Black
Step 2: Backstitch (1 strand)		
403		310 Black
Step 3: French Knots (1 strand)		
46	●	1017 Christmas Red-bright (Marlitt)

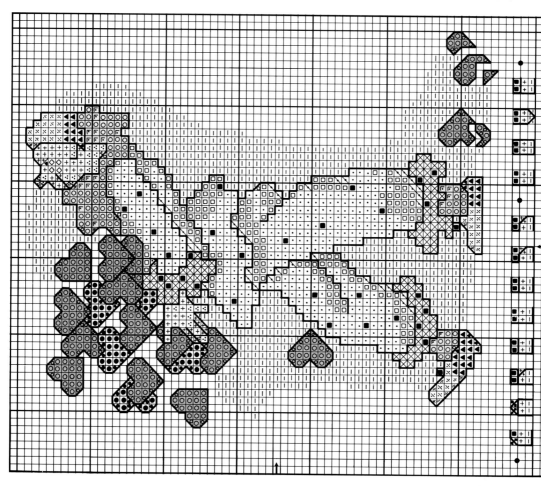

Stitch Count: 56 x 69 (Careless Love)

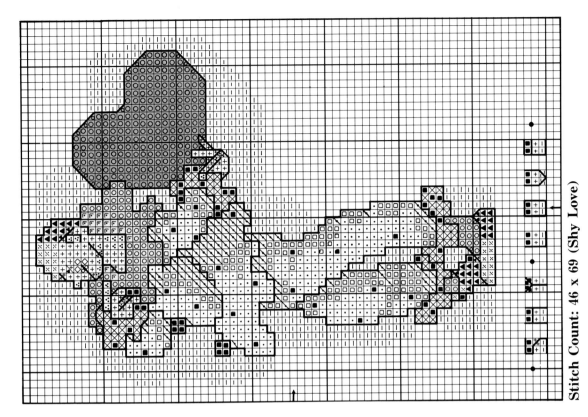

Stitch Count: 46 x 69 (Shy Love)

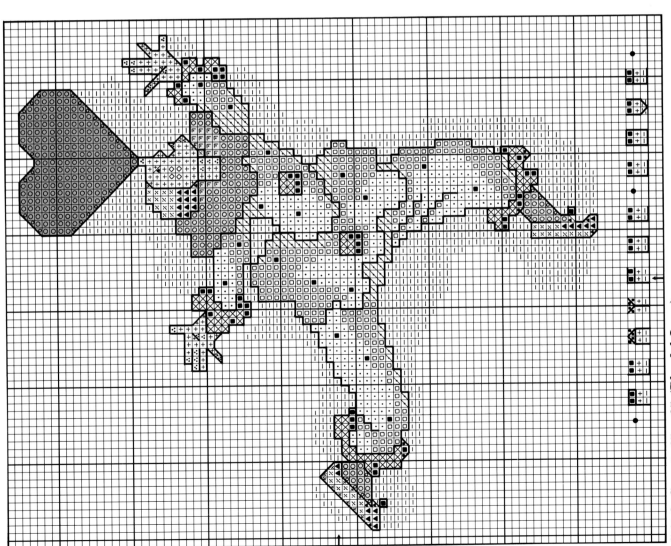

Stitch Count: 65 x 85 (Playful Love)

Heartfelt Valentine Sentiments

SAMPLE for Love Card
Stitched on white Perforated Paper 14, the finished design size is 10″ x 2½″. The paper was cut 12″ x 14″. See instructions before stitching.

MATERIALS
Completed cross-stitch on white Perforated Paper 14
1 (9″ x 5″) piece of pink paper
10½″ (¾″-wide) mauve grosgrain ribbon
10¾″ (½″-wide) white lace trim
¾ yard (⅛″-wide) burgundy silk ribbon
1¼ yards (¼″-wide) green silk ribbon
White glue
Large-eyed needle

FABRICS	DESIGN SIZES
Aida 11	12¾″ x 3⅛″
Aida 14	10″ x 2½″
Aida 18	7¾″ x 2″
Hardanger 22	6⅜″ x 1⅝″

DIRECTIONS

1. Referring to Diagrams A and B, draw outline of card on un-stitched perforated paper with a pencil, using Diagram B to count number of holes in each scallop. Referring to Diagram B for placement, stitch "LOVE" design on perforated paper. Cut out card.

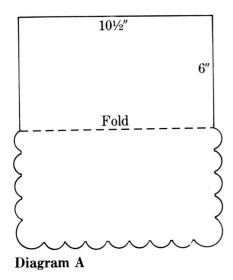

Diagram A

10½″

6″

Fold

2. Fold card where indicated (Diagram A). Place card on a protected surface. Apply glue sparingly to back of pink paper, center it on inside back of perforated card, and press in place. Let glue dry.

3. Open card and lay flat. Fold under ends of mauve ribbon ¼″. Apply glue sparingly to back of ribbon and press in place on front of card, below stitching (Diagram B). Fold under ends of lace ½″. Apply glue sparingly to back of lace and center it on top of mauve ribbon. Press in place. Let glue dry.

4. Thread needle with burgundy ribbon. Thread ribbon through 2 holes in 1 scallop (Diagram B). Knot ribbon close to surface of paper. Trim ribbon ends to ¼″. Repeat for remaining scallops. Wrap green ribbon around card and tie a bow in corner (see photo).

SAMPLE for Heart Gift Tag
Stitched on white Perforated Paper 14, the finished design size is 3″ x 2⅝″. The paper was cut 5″ x 5″. Stitch the motif in the center of the paper.

FABRICS	DESIGN SIZES
Aida 11	3⅞″ x 3¼″
Aida 14	3″ x 2⅝″
Aida 18	2⅜″ x 2″
Hardanger 22	1⅞″ x 1⅝″

MATERIALS
Completed cross-stitch on white Perforated Paper 14
1 (⅝″ x 3¼″) piece of heavy paper for tag
Craft knife

DIRECTIONS

1. To make heart shape, cut paper 1 hole outside stitching, around entire design (edge will be irregular).

2. Trace and cut out tag pattern. Place pattern on heavy paper and cut out. Print "To My Valentine" on tag. Decorate tag as desired.

3. Using craft knife, cut a ⅜″ slit in center of heart. Insert tab in slit and fold back to hold in place.

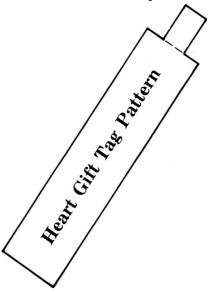

Heart Gift Tag Pattern

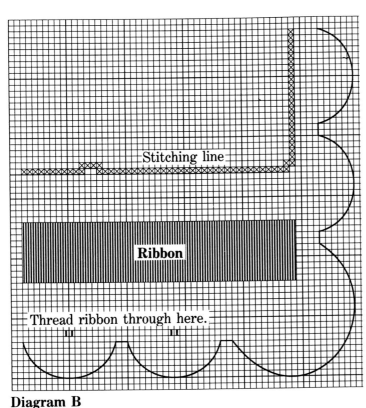

Stitching line

Ribbon

Thread ribbon through here.

Diagram B

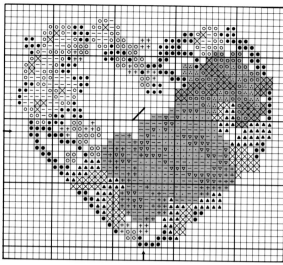

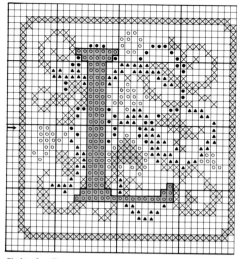

Stitch Count: 42 x 36 (Heart Gift Tag)

Stitch Count: 140 x 35 (Love Card)

SAMPLE for I Love You Card

Stitched on white Perforated Paper 14, the finished design size is 5½" x 3⅞". The paper was cut 9" x 7". Stitch the motif in the center of the paper.

FABRICS	DESIGN SIZES
Aida 11	6⅞" x 4⅞"
Aida 14	5½" x 3⅞"
Aida 18	4¼" x 3"
Hardanger 22	3½" x 2½"

MATERIALS

Completed cross-stitch on white
  Perforated Paper 14
1 (9" x 7") piece of unstitched
  Perforated Paper 14
1 (6" x 4") piece of pink paper

1 yard (⅛"-wide) pink silk ribbon
1 yard (⅛"-wide) red silk ribbon
1 yard (⅛"-wide) lavender silk
  ribbon
White glue
Large-eyed needle
Tracing paper

DIRECTIONS

1. Transfer heart pattern on next page to tracing paper and cut out. On back of design piece, lightly trace heart pattern with a pencil. Also trace heart onto piece of un-stitched perforated paper for back of card. Cut out hearts.

2. Cut pink paper heart 2" smaller than perforated paper heart. Apply glue sparingly to back of pink heart and position it where desired on inside back of perforated card. Press in place. Let glue dry.

3. Place the 2 perforated paper hearts together with the pink heart inside.

4. Trim each length of ribbon to 32". Thread large-eyed needle with the 3 ribbons. Referring to heart pattern for placement, insert nee-dle down through upper left edge of hearts, then up through lower left edge. With ribbon ends even and holding them together as 1, tie in a bow.

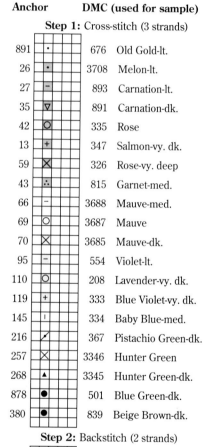

Anchor		DMC	(used for sample)
Step 1: Cross-stitch (3 strands)			
891	·	676	Old Gold-lt.
26	•	3708	Melon-lt.
27	–	893	Carnation-lt.
35	▽	891	Carnation-dk.
42	O	335	Rose
13	+	347	Salmon-vy. dk.
59	X	326	Rose-vy. deep
43	∴	815	Garnet-med.
66	–	3688	Mauve-med.
69	O	3687	Mauve
70	X	3685	Mauve-dk.
95	–	554	Violet-lt.
110	O	208	Lavender-vy. dk.
119	+	333	Blue Violet-vy. dk.
145	¦	334	Baby Blue-med.
216	/	367	Pistachio Green-dk.
257	X	3346	Hunter Green
268	▲	3345	Hunter Green-dk.
878	●	501	Blue Green-dk.
380	●	839	Beige Brown-dk.
Step 2: Backstitch (2 strands)			
59		326	Rose-vy. deep (arrow going in and out on hearts)
70		3685	Mauve-dk. (L-O-V-E letters)
878		501	Blue Green-dk. ("I Love You," stems)
309		435	Brown-vy. lt. (arrow)
Step 3: Cut Slit			

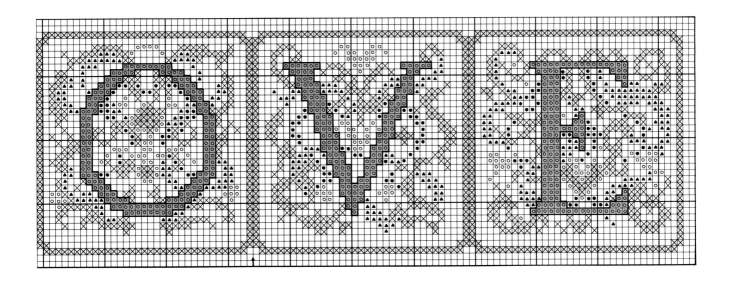

Pattern for I Love You Card

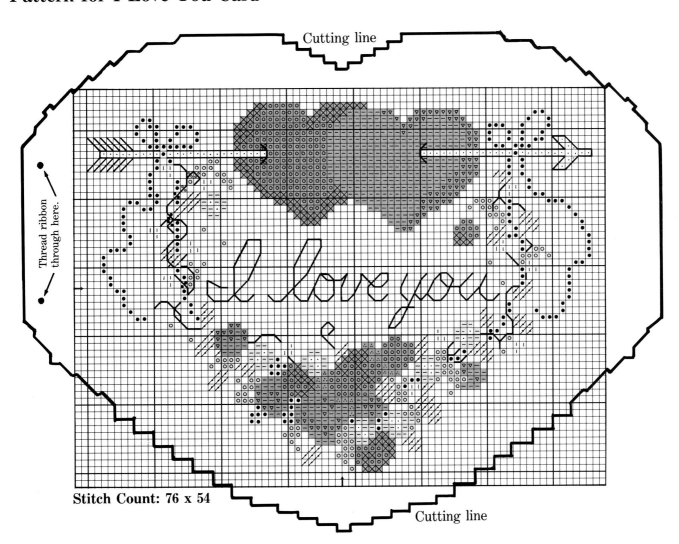

Stitch Count: 76 x 54

Cutting line

Cutting line

Thread ribbon through here.

MARCH 17
St. Patrick's Day

It's March 17th, so don't forget to wear your green! Dress your table for the occasion, too, with this shamrock-trimmed table-cloth. It's the perfect pinch of green for your St. Patrick's Day feast.

Tablecloth

SAMPLE

Stitched on white Belfast Linen 32 over 2 threads, the finished design size is 7¾″ x 7¼″ for 1 motif. The fabric was cut 56″ x 54″. Begin stitching the first motif 4″ from the lower edge of fabric, centering the design horizontally. Repeat the motif once on each side of the center motif as indicated by heavy lines. Repeat on remaining 3 sides of tablecloth (see photo).

MATERIALS

Completed cross-stitch on white Belfast Linen 32
Matching thread

DIRECTIONS

To hem, fold raw edges of linen under 1⅛″ twice and press. Machine-hemstitch.

Option: A napkin can be made by stitching 1 shamrock and the 3 flowers below shamrock on an 18″ x 16½″ piece of white Belfast Linen 32. Begin stitching bottom row of design 2¼″ from napkin's lower edge, centering the design horizontally. To hem napkin, fold raw edges under ½″ twice and press. Machine-hemstitch.

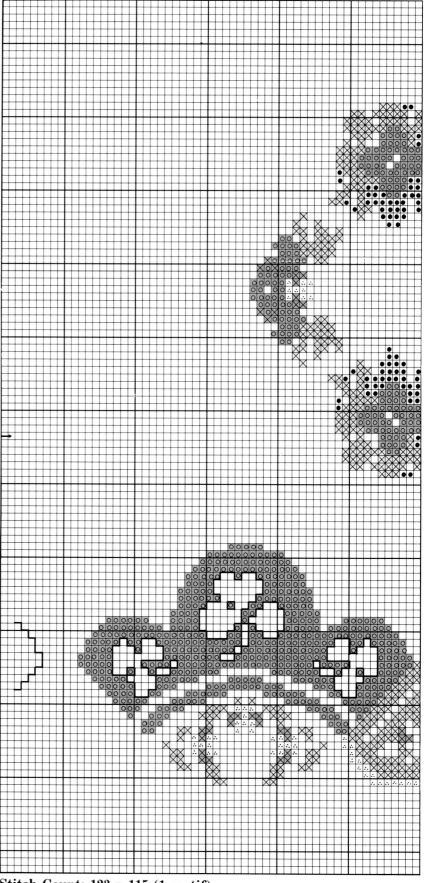

Stitch Count: 123 x 115 (1 motif)

Anchor		DMC (used for sample)	
Step 1: Cross-stitch (2 strands)			
4146	∴	754	Peach-lt.
8	⊠	353	Peach
870	⊙	3042	Antique Violet-lt.
167	●	597	Turquoise
213	⊠	369	Pistachio Green-vy. lt.
215	⊙	320	Pistachio Green-med.
Step 2: Backstitch (1 strand)			
215		320	Pistachio Green-med.

MARCH 20
Kite Festival

Spend a relaxing March day catching just the right breeze and send your spirits soaring. These miniature box kites embellished with special stitching, threads, and beads may not take flight, but they will pass with flying colors as decorations for almost any room!

Box Kites

SAMPLE for Kite #1
Stitched on cracked wheat Murano 30 over 1 thread, the finished design size is ½″ x ⅜″ for 1 repeat. For complete kite, cut 2 (5″ x 10″) pieces of fabric.

On each piece, begin stitching design 2¼″ below top edge and ½″ from left edge of fabric. Complete top row of long stitches, working stitches that are over 2 vertical threads, 3, 2, 1, and so on. Continue stitching top row to within ½″ of right edge of fabric. Return to left edge to stitch second row, beginning with stitch that is over 2 vertical threads, 1, 2, 3, and so on. Stitch third row, beginning with 1 stitch over 1 vertical thread, then skipping 2 threads and stitching 2 single stitches. Complete with second color.

FABRICS	DESIGN SIZES
Aida 11	1½″ x 1⅛″
Aida 14	1⅛″ x ⅞″
Aida 18	⅞″ x ⅝″
Hardanger 22	¾″ x ½″

SAMPLE for Kite #2
Stitched on cracked wheat Murano 30 over 2 threads, the finished design size is 1½″ x ⅝″ for 1 repeat. For complete kite, cut 2 (5″ x 10″) pieces of fabric. On each piece, begin ½″ from left edge, center motif and repeat horizontally across fabric as indicated by the heavy lines, to within ½″ of right edge.

FABRICS	DESIGN SIZES
Aida 11	2⅛″ x ⅞″
Aida 14	1⅝″ x ¾″
Aida 18	1¼″ x ½″
Hardanger 22	1″ x ½″

SAMPLE for Kite #3
Stitched on celery green Linda 27 over 2 threads, the finished design size is 1⅛″ x 1⅛″ for 1 repeat. For complete kite, cut 2 (5″ x 10″) pieces of fabric. On each piece, begin ½″ from left edge, center motif and repeat horizontally across fabric as indicated by heavy lines, to within ½″ of right edge.

FABRICS	DESIGN SIZES
Aida 11	1⅜″ x 1⅜″
Aida 14	1⅛″ x 1⅛″
Aida 18	⅞″ x ⅞″
Hardanger 22	⅝″ x ⅝″

SAMPLE for Kite #4
Stitched on white Quaker Cloth 28 over 2 threads, the finished design size is 1⅞″ x ⅝″ for 1 repeat. For complete kite, cut 2 (5″ x 10″) pieces of fabric. On each piece, begin ½″ from left edge, center motif and repeat horizontally across fabric as indicated by heavy lines, to within ½″ of right edge.

FABRICS	DESIGN SIZES
Aida 11	2⅜″ x ¾″
Aida 14	1⅞″ x ⅝″
Aida 18	1½″ x ½″
Hardanger 22	1⅛″ x ⅜″

SAMPLE for Kite #5
Stitched on white Belfast Linen 32 over 2 threads, the finished design size is 2″ x 1¼″ for 1 repeat. For complete kite, cut 2 (5″ x 10″) pieces of fabric. On each piece, begin ½″ from left edge, center motif and repeat horizontally across fabric as indicated by heavy lines, to within ½″ of right edge.

FABRICS	DESIGN SIZES
Aida 11	2⅞″ x 1¾″
Aida 14	2¼″ x 1⅜″
Aida 18	1¾″ x 1″
Hardanger 22	1⅜″ x ⅞″

SAMPLE for Kite #6
Stitched on pewter Murano 30 over 2 threads, the finished design size is ¾″ x ⅝″ for 1 repeat. For complete kite, cut 2 (5″ x 10″) pieces of fabric. On each piece, begin ½″ from left edge, center motif and repeat horizontally across fabric as indicated by heavy lines, to within ½″ of right edge.

FABRICS	DESIGN SIZES
Aida 11	1″ x ⅞″
Aida 14	¾″ x ¾″
Aida 18	⅝″ x ½″
Hardanger 22	½″ x ½″

SAMPLE for Kite #7
Stitched on cream Belfast Linen 32 over 2 threads, the finished design size is 1¼″ x ¾″ for 1 repeat. For complete kite, cut 2 (5″ x 10″) pieces of fabric. On each piece, begin ½″ from left edge, center motif and repeat horizontally across fabric as indicated by heavy lines, to within ½″ of right edge.

FABRICS	DESIGN SIZES
Aida 11	1¾″ x 1″
Aida 14	1⅜″ x ¾″
Aida 18	1″ x ⅝″
Hardanger 22	⅞″ x ½″

SAMPLE for Kite #8
Stitched on white Murano 30 over 2 threads, the finished design size is 1″ x ⅝″ for 1 repeat. For complete kite, cut 2 (5″ x 10″) pieces of fabric. On each piece, begin ½″ from left edge, center motif, and repeat horizontally across fabric as indicated by heavy lines, to within ½″ of right edge.

FABRICS	DESIGN SIZES
Aida 11	1⅜″ x ⅞″
Aida 14	1⅛″ x ⅝″
Aida 18	⅞″ x ½″
Hardanger 22	⅝″ x ⅜″

Note: See Suppliers for Mill Hill Beads and special threads.

Kite #1

Marlitt (used for sample)

Step 1: Long Stitch (1 strand)

 1001 Peach Beige

1059 Blue-vy. lt.

Kite #2

DMC (used for sample)

Step 1: Cross-stitch (2 strands)

 3350 Dusty Rose-vy. dk.

943 Aquamarine-med.

Kite #3

DMC (used for sample)

Step 1: Cross-stitch (2 strands)

 991 Aquamarine-dk. (1 strand) +
009 Emerald High Luster Balger
blending filament (1 strand)

Step 2: Satin stitch (1 strand)

 703 Chartreuse

Step 3: Beadwork

 00968 Red

Kite #4

DMC (used for sample)

Step 1: Cross-stitch (2 strands)

 744 Yellow-pale

309 Rose-deep

Step 2: Scotch Stitch (1 strand)

 309 Rose-deep

807 Peacock Blue

Step 3: Beadwork

 02005 Dusty Rose

02008 Sea Breeze

Step 4: Long Stitch (1 strand)

 211 Emotion Wild Threads

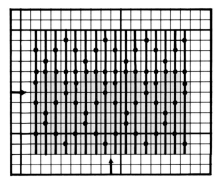

Kite #1

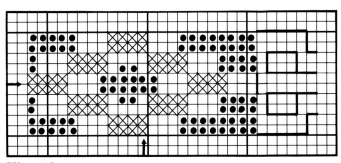

Kite #2

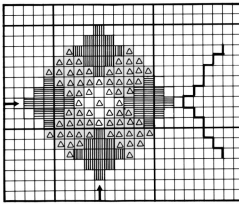

Kite #3

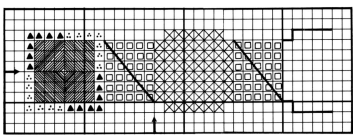

Kite #4

Kite #5

Floss (used for sample)

Step 1: Satin Stitch (1 strand)

 1066　Aquamarine-lt. (Marlitt)

Step 2: Long Stitch (1 strand)

 708　Savage Wild Threads

Step 3: Beadwork

 02008　Sea Breeze

Kite #6

Floss (used for sample)

Step 1: Long Stitch (1 strand)

 901　Strip Wild Threads

Step 2: Beadwork

 00081　Jet

Kite #7

Marlitt (used for sample)

Step 1: Cross-stitch (2 strands)

 1007　Lavender-lt.

　　　 858　Violet-dk.

　　　 1053　Wedgewood-lt.

Step 2: Ribbonwork

 Hunter Green ribbon
(1/16" wide) (bring ribbon up
and down at ends of square)

Kite #8

DMC (used for sample)

Step 1: Cross-stitch (2 strands)

 353　Peach (DMC)

Step 2: Scotch Stitch (1 strand)

 836　Royal Blue (over 6 threads)
(Marlitt)

　　　 836　Royal Blue (over 6 threads)
(Marlitt)

Step 3: Beadwork

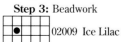 02009　Ice Lilac

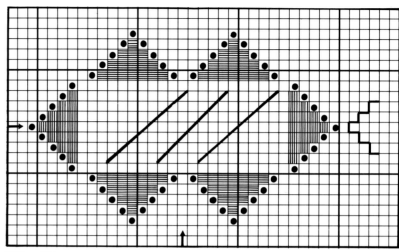

Kite #5

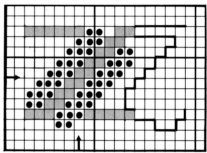

Kite #6

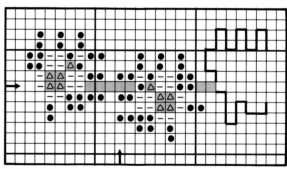

Kite #7

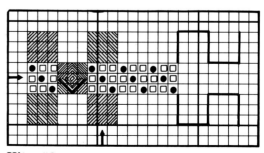

Kite #8

MATERIALS (for 1 kite)

Completed cross-stitch; matching thread
1 skein Marlitt in a matching color
2 (36″) lengths of ⅛″ dowel
Wood glue
Craft knife

DIRECTIONS

All seam allowances are ¼″.

1. To construct kite frame, cut 4 (4½″) lengths, 8 (2″) lengths, and 2 (2¾″) lengths from dowels. To make top square of frame, glue ends of 4 (2″) dowels together to make a square; repeat to make bottom square of frame. To support squares, whittle end of 2¾″ length to form a wedge. Repeat for other end. Glue in place diagonally across each square. Finish frame by gluing 1 (4½″) dowel to each corner of top and bottom squares (see Diagram).

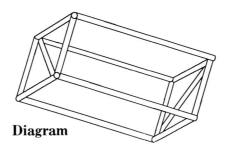

Diagram

2. From skein of Marlitt, cut 1 (30″) piece for kite string. To cover dowels, wrap remaining Marlitt tightly around entire frame, securing at each corner by wrapping 2-3 layers tightly over corner and gluing in place.

3. With right sides facing, fold 1 design piece in half lengthwise. Stitch together along long edge. Trim seam allowance. Turn. Fold so that seam is centered on back. Press. Fold under ¼″ on 1 end. Slip raw end inside folded end. Pin in place. Repeat for remaining design piece. Slip 1 design piece over coordinating frame top, and 1 over bottom. Adjust design pieces as needed by pulling ends together to fit snugly. Slipstitch ends together. Attach (30″) Marlitt for string. Tie as shown (see photo).

MARCH 21
Fragrance Day

The aroma of fresh rose petals. A pine forest after a rain. Cherry blossoms in the spring. These are just a few of the delightful fragrances we too-often fail to enjoy as we hurry through life. The delicate floral cross-stitch of our matching coverlet and pillow may help recall some of these favorite fragrances.

Quilt

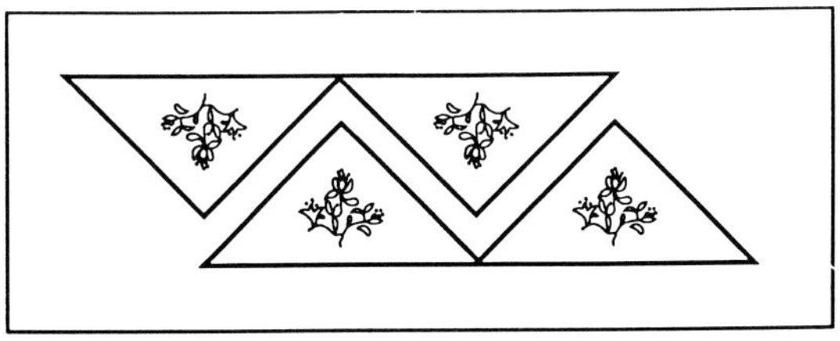

Diagram A

SAMPLE

Stitched on white Hardanger 22 over 2 threads, finished design size is 4⅜″ x 4″. Finished size of the completed quilt is 38½″ x 49½″. Mark 4 triangles on fabric before stitching (see Step 1 of Directions).

FABRICS	DESIGN SIZES
Aida 11	4⅜″ x 4″
Aida 14	3⅜″ x 3⅛″
Aida 18	2⅝″ x 2½″
Hardanger 22	2⅛″ x 2″

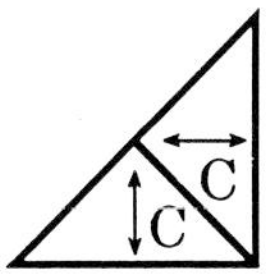

Diagram B

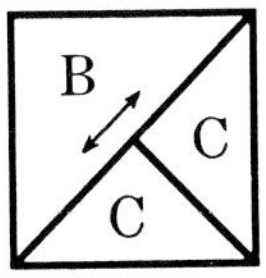

Diagram C

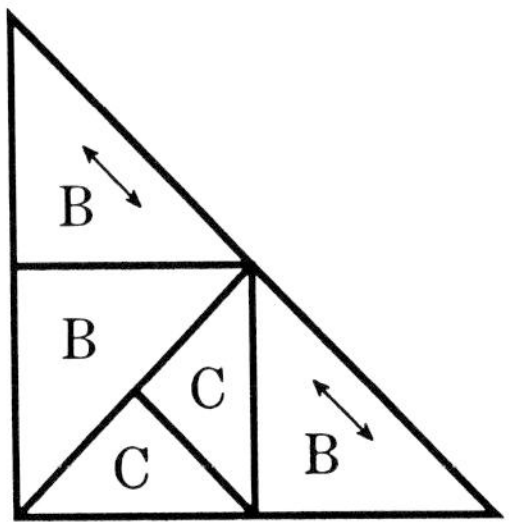

Diagram D

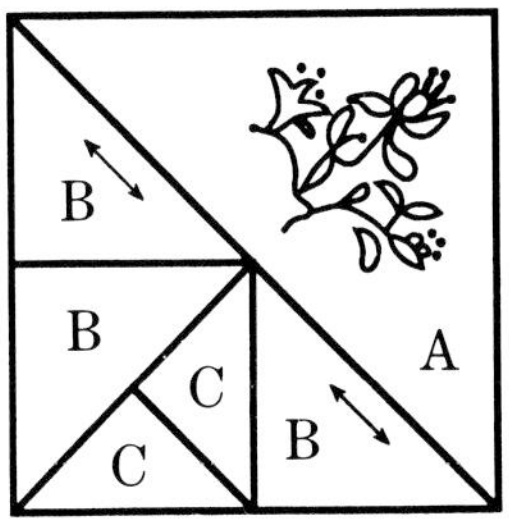

Diagram E

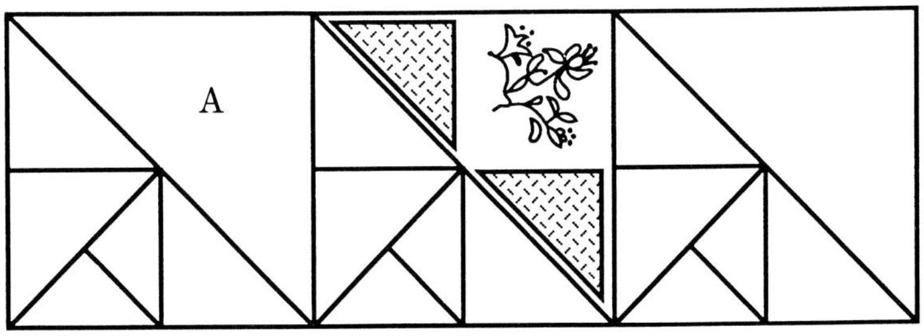

Diagram F

MATERIALS

1 (12″ x 50″) piece of white Hardanger 22; matching thread
1½ yards (45″-wide) white fabric (for backing)
2 yards (45″-wide) white fabric with ¼″ tucks (available with wedding fabrics)
1 yard (45″-wide) blue print fabric; matching thread
1½ yards (45″-wide) polyester batting
White quilting thread
Dressmakers' pen
Frosted vinyl or lightweight cardboard

DIRECTIONS

All seam allowances are ¼″, except where indicated.

1. Transfer patterns for quilt to template material and cut out. Trace triangle A onto Hardanger 4 times, noting grain line (see Diagram A). Do not cut out. Cross-stitch design, centering bottom cross-stitch horizontally 1¾″ from long edge of triangle. Cut out triangles.

2. Cut 1 (40½″ x 51½″) piece from white for backing. (Piece is 2″ longer and wider than finished size to allow for take-up during quilting.) Cut the following pieces from tucked fabric, noting grain line: 8 triangle As, 36 triangle Bs, and 24 triangle Cs. Also cut 2 (2¾″ x 35¾″) and 2 (2¾″ x 46¾″) strips for borders. Cut batting 40½″ x 51½″.

3. From blue print, cut 8 triangle Cs. Cut a 2¼″-wide bias strip for binding, piecing as needed to equal 5 yards. Also cut a 1¼″-wide bias strip for bows, piecing as needed to equal 3 yards.

4. To form a block, with right sides facing and raw edges aligned, stitch short sides of 2 tucked triangle Cs together (see Diagram B). Join a triangle B to form a small square (see Diagram C). Then join triangle Bs to 2 sides of square, forming a triangle (see Diagram D). Join Hardanger design piece to this triangle to complete block (see Diagram E). Repeat to make 3 more blocks. Then, replacing the design piece with triangle As of white tucked fabric, make 8 additional blocks in this manner.

5. Turn under ⅛″ seam allowance on 2 blue print triangle Cs and place them ½″ from side and ¼″ from bottom seams at corners of 1 Hardanger triangle. Appliqué to Hardanger. Repeat with remaining blue triangles.

6. To make Row 1 of quilt, join 2 white blocks and 1 design block as shown, keeping triangle A in upper right-hand corner of each block (see Diagram F). For Row 2, rotate blocks ¼ turn so that triangle A is in upper left corner (see Quilt Diagram). Make Row 3 to match Row 1 and Row 4 to match Row 2. Join rows.

7. To attach border to quilt top, start at upper right corner and place 1 (2¾″ x 35¾″) strip along top edge of quilt, with right sides facing and right end of strip aligned with right edge of quilt. Stitch to within 1″ of upper left corner. Turn border to right side and press seam to 1 side. To attach right border, with right sides facing, align 1 (2¾″ x 46¾″) strip with lower right corner and stitch along entire right edge, joining right border to top border. Turn border to right side and press seam to 1 side. Add bottom border and then left border in same manner. Return to top border strip. Fold corner of top strip down again and stitch upper left corner, joining top border to left border (see Quilt Diagram).

8. Stack layers in this order: backing (right side down); batting; top (right side up). Baste the 3 layers together from the center out. Quilt with white thread ¼″ inside seam line on each design piece, diagonally through each block along seam lines and through center of white As (but not design pieces), and ¼″ inside binding. Trim batting.

9. Trim to round corners of quilt slightly. To bind edges, with right sides facing and raw edges aligned, stitch 2¼″-wide bias strip to quilt top with a ½″ seam. Fold strip to back of quilt, easing corners. Turn under ½″ along raw edge of strip and slipstitch folded edge to back of quilt.

10. To make bows, fold under ¼″ on each long edge of 1¼″-wide bias strip. Then fold in half lengthwise with long raw edges to inside. Topstitch folded edges together. Cut strip into 4 (27″) lengths. Tie each length into a bow. Center 1 bow between appliquéd triangles on each Hardanger triangle and tack securely. Knot ends of bows.

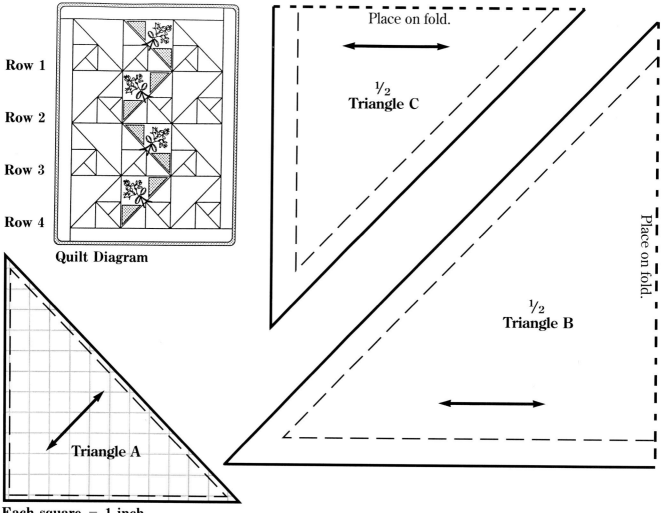

Quilt Diagram

Place on fold.

½
Triangle C

½
Triangle B

Place on fold.

Triangle A

Each square = 1 inch.

Pillow

SAMPLE

Stitched on white Hardanger 22 over 2 threads, the finished design size is 4⅜″ x 4″. Mark a triangle on the fabric before stitching (see Step 1 of Directions).

MATERIALS

1 (11½″-square) piece of Hardanger 22; matching thread
½ yard (45″-wide) white fabric with ¼″ tucks (available with wedding fabrics)
1 (16¼″-square) piece of white flannel
¼ yard (45″-wide) blue print fabric; matching thread
1 (18″) square pillow form
Dressmakers' pen
Frosted vinyl or lightweight cardboard
White quilting thread

DIRECTIONS

1. Transfer patterns to template material and cut out. Trace triangle A onto Hardanger, noting grain line. Cross-stitch design, centering bottom cross-stitch horizontally 1¾″ from long edge of triangle. Cut out triangle.

2. Cut the following pieces from tucked fabric, noting grain line: 3 triangle Bs, 2 triangle Cs, 4 (3″ x 14″) strips for border, and 1 (17″) square for pillow back.

3. From blue print, cut 2 triangle Cs. Cut a 1¼″-wide bias strip for the bow, piecing as needed to equal 27″.

4. Refer to Step 4 of quilt to make 1 block.

5. Refer to Step 5 of quilt to appliqué blue print triangles.

6. Refer to Step 7 of the quilt to attach the borders to the pillow front, as shown in Diagram G below.

Diagram G

7. Baste flannel square to wrong side of pillow front. Quilt ¼″ inside all seam lines of Hardanger and in the border ¾″ outside block.

8. With right sides facing, stitch front to back, leaving a large opening on 1 side. Trim seams, clip corners, and turn right side out. Insert pillow form. Slipstitch opening closed.

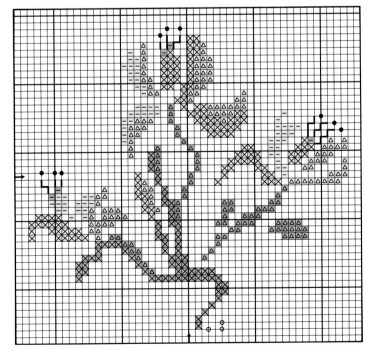

Stitch Count: 48 x 44

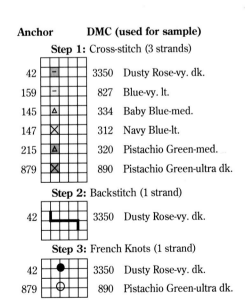

Anchor		DMC (used for sample)	
	Step 1: Cross-stitch (3 strands)		
42	–	3350	Dusty Rose-vy. dk.
159	–	827	Blue-vy. lt.
145	△	334	Baby Blue-med.
147	X	312	Navy Blue-lt.
215	▲	320	Pistachio Green-med.
879	X	890	Pistachio Green-ultra dk.
	Step 2: Backstitch (1 strand)		
42		3350	Dusty Rose-vy. dk.
	Step 3: French Knots (1 strand)		
42	●	3350	Dusty Rose-vy. dk.
879	⊕	890	Pistachio Green-ultra dk.

National Bubblegum Week

The celebration of this week originated with the idea that students studying for final exams could combat stress by chewing "bubble-blowing, tension-breaking" gum. The free distribution of bubblegum during finals week was encouraged. We encourage it with this design, stitched in bright bubblegum colors.

Bubblegum Sampler

Stitch Count: 186 x 104

SAMPLE

Stitched on white Linda 27 over 2 threads, the finished design size is 13¾″ x 7¾″. Fabric was cut 20″ x 14″. See Suppliers for Mill Hill Beads.

FABRICS	DESIGN SIZES
Aida 11	16⅞″ x 9½″
Aida 14	13¼″ x 7⅜″
Aida 18	10⅜″ x 5¾″
Hardanger 22	8½″ x 4¾″

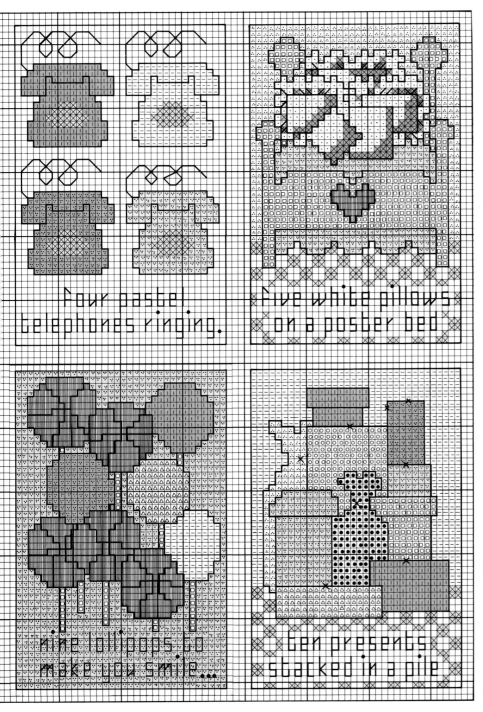

Anchor		DMC (used for sample)

Step 1: Cross-stitch (2 strands)

Anchor		DMC	
1	·		White
297	∴	743	Yellow-med.
50	∴	605	Cranberry-vy. lt.
46	△	666	Christmas Red-bright
88	●	718	Plum
130	−	809	Delft
978	○	322	Navy Blue-vy. lt.
186	I	959	Seagreen-med.
923	∴	699	Christmas Green
308	□	976	Golden Brown-med.
398	⊠	415	Pearl Gray
399	▽	318	Steel Gray-lt.
403	⊠	310	Black

Step 2: Satin Stitch (1 strand)

1	‖‖‖		White (see photo)
46	‖‖‖	666	Christmas Red-bright (see photo)
308	‖‖‖	976	Golden Brown-med. (hatband)

Step 3: Tufting (3 strands)

308	■	976	Golden Brown-med. (For each stitch, backstitch over 1 thread; working over the backstitch, make a loop stitch about ⅛″ deep. Continue stitching to fill area, then clip all loops.)

Step 4: Backstitch (1 strand)

403	L	310	Black (2 strands) (phone cords, yellow cone hat)
403	L	310	Black (all else)

Step 5: French Knots (1 strand)

403	●	310	Black

Step 6: Beadwork

S	00148	Pale Peach
R	00968	Red
U	00146	Lt. Blue
H	00431	Jade Green

Step 7: Ribbons and Bows (see photo) (¹/₁₆″ wide ribbon)

✗	White Ribbon (blue box, seagreen box)
✗	Yellow Pearl Cotton #8 (green box, plum box)
✗	Red Ribbon (pink box)
✗	Green Ribbon (red box, small yellow box)
✗	Black Pearl Cotton #8 (baskets)

43

Easter

The rabbit has long been a symbol of Easter. This custom is believed to stem from the story of Eostre, the ancient goddess of spring and fertility, who was represented by the hare. We bet the hare wasn't as cute as these bunnies. They'll make a sweet carriage coverlet and pillows for the Easter parade.

Bunny Pillows

SAMPLES
Stitched on white Gardasee 14, the finished design sizes are: 2¾″ x 3¼″ for the flower, 3⅛″ x 3⅝″ for the umbrella, 3″ x 3⅛″ for the basket, and 2¾″ x 3¼″ for the bear. The fabric was cut 8″ x 16″ for each pillow.

Flower
FABRICS	DESIGN SIZES
Aida 11	3½″ x 4⅛″
Aida 14	2¾″ x 3¼″
Aida 18	2⅛″ x 2½″
Hardanger 22	1¾″ x 2″

Umbrella
FABRICS	DESIGN SIZES
Aida 11	4″ x 4⅝″
Aida 14	3⅛″ x 3⅝″
Aida 18	2⅜″ x 2⅞″
Hardanger 22	2″ x 2⅜″

Basket
FABRICS	DESIGN SIZES
Aida 11	3⅞″ x 4″
Aida 14	3″ x 3⅛″
Aida 18	2⅛″ x 2½″
Hardanger 22	1⅞″ x 2″

Bear
FABRICS	DESIGN SIZES
Aida 11	3½″ x 4⅛″
Aida 14	2¾″ x 3¼″
Aida 18	2⅛″ x 2½″
Hardanger 22	1¾″ x 2⅛″

MATERIALS (for 1 pillow)
Completed cross-stitch on white Gardasee 14
¼ yard (45″-wide) purple print fabric for binding; matching thread
½ yard (45″-wide) fabric for pillow; matching thread
2 yards of matching ribbon
Stuffing

DIRECTIONS
1. With design centered, trim Gardasee to 6½″ x 14″. From purple print fabric, cut 2⅛″-wide bias strips, piecing as needed, to equal 44″. Cut bias strips into 2 (7″) lengths and 2 (15″) lengths. Cut 2 (12″ x 19″) pieces from the pillow fabric.

2. To bind edges of design piece, with right sides facing and raw edges aligned, pin 1 (7″) bias strip to 1 end of design piece. Stitch with ½″ seam. Trim ends of strip even with design piece. Fold under ½″ on remaining long edge of bias strip and fold over to wrong side of design piece. Slipstitch folded edge in place. Repeat with second 7″

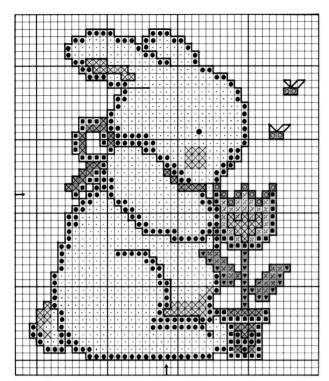

Stitch Count: 39 x 45 (flower)

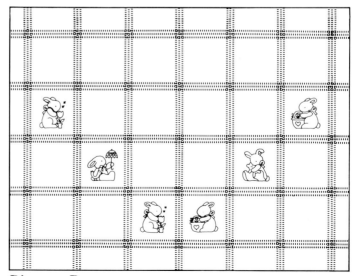

Stitch Count: 42 x 44 (basket)

strip on opposite end of design piece. In same manner, attach 1 (15″) bias strip to side of design piece. Fold under ends of strip so that they are even with edge of design piece. Stitch with ½″ seam. Fold strip and slipstitch in place as above. Repeat with second 15″ strip on opposite side.

3. To attach ribbons to design piece for ties, cut ribbon into 6 (12″) lengths. Make a 1″ loop on 1 end of each ribbon. With design piece right side up, pin loops of 3 ribbons to binding across each end of design piece (see Diagram A). Stitch in place.

4. Place right sides of pillow pieces together. Stitch with ¼″ seam, leaving a 3″ opening for turning. Clip corners and turn right side out. Stuff. Slipstitch opening closed.

5. Wrap design piece around center of pillow and tie ribbons in back, drawing center of pillow in slightly.

Coverlet

SAMPLE

Stitched on white Undine 14, the finished design sizes are the same as for the pillows. The fabric was cut 38″ x 57″ for the coverlet. See Diagram B for placement of the designs.

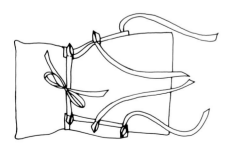

Diagram A

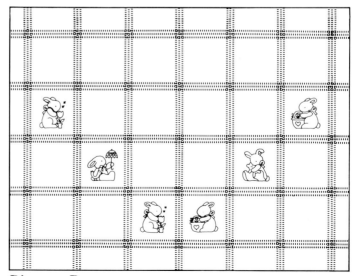

Diagram B

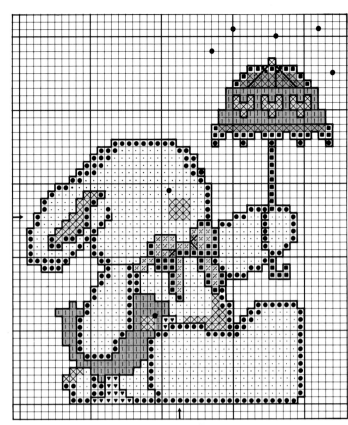

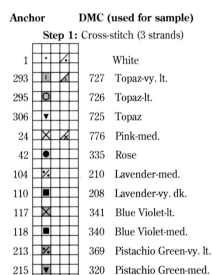

Stitch Count: 43 x 51 (umbrella)

Stitch Count: 39 x 46 (bear)

MATERIALS
Completed cross-stitch on Undine 14
¾ yard (45″-wide) purple print
fabric for binding; matching
thread

DIRECTIONS
1. Cut 2⅛″-wide bias strips from
print fabric, piecing as needed to
make 5½ yards.

2. To bind edges, with right sides
facing and raw edges aligned, pin
strip along edges of design piece.
Stitch with ½″ seam, stopping ½″
from corner; backstitch (see Diagram C). Fold strip at right angle
to turn corner (see Diagram D).
Resume stitching with backstitch
½″ from corner along adjacent
edge. Repeat at each corner.

3. Fold under ½″ on remaining
raw edge of bias strip and fold to
wrong side, making binding. Slipstitch in place, covering stitching
line and easing fabric at corners.
Slipstitch folds in place.

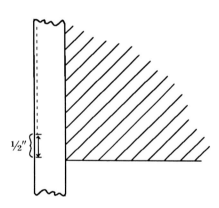

½″

Diagram C

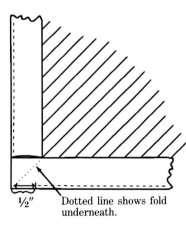

½″ Dotted line shows fold
underneath.

Diagram D

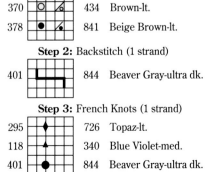

Anchor			DMC (used for sample)
			Step 1: Cross-stitch (3 strands)
1	·	∕	White
293	I	∕	727 Topaz-vy. lt.
295	O		726 Topaz-lt.
306	▼		725 Topaz
24	✕	⊠	776 Pink-med.
42	●		335 Rose
104	⁒		210 Lavender-med.
110	■		208 Lavender-vy. dk.
117	✕		341 Blue Violet-lt.
118	■		340 Blue Violet-med.
213	⁒		369 Pistachio Green-vy. lt.
215	▼		320 Pistachio Green-med.
363	I	∕	436 Tan
370	O	∕	434 Brown-lt.
378	●	∕	841 Beige Brown-lt.
			Step 2: Backstitch (1 strand)
401			844 Beaver Gray-ultra dk.
			Step 3: French Knots (1 strand)
295	◆		726 Topaz-lt.
118	▲		340 Blue Violet-med.
401	●		844 Beaver Gray-ultra dk.

APRIL 2
Blessing of the Animals

This holiday is dedicated to "all creatures, great and small." Our playful silhouette depicts a delightful harmony between a boy and his friends, reminding us that we all share this world.

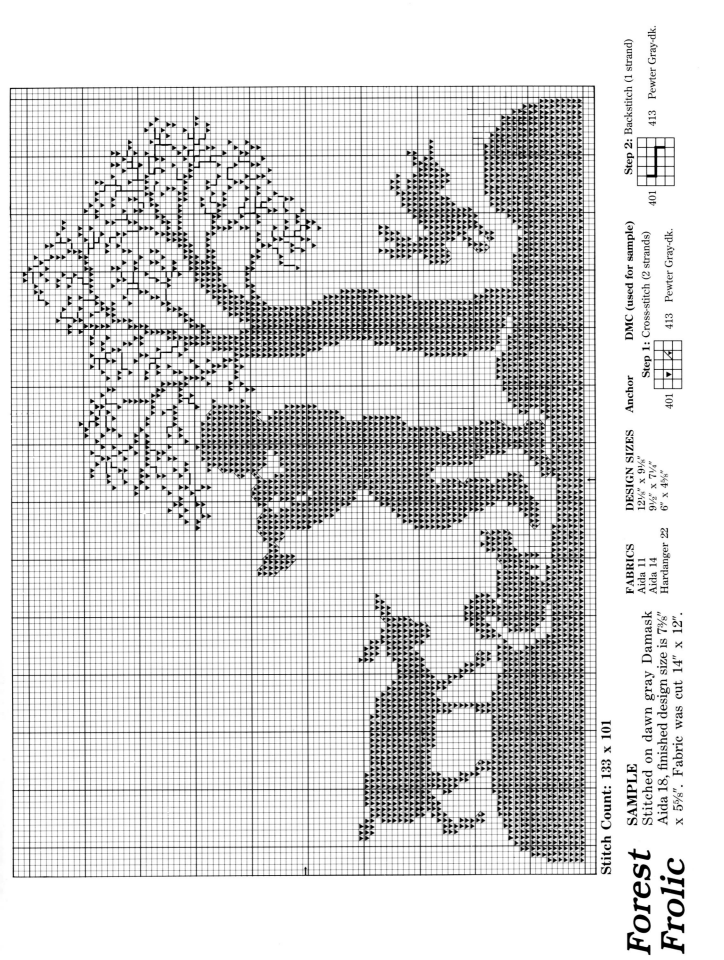

Stitch Count: 133 x 101

Forest Frolic

SAMPLE
Stitched on dawn gray Damask
Aida 18, finished design size is 7⅜"
x 5⅝". Fabric was cut 14" x 12".

FABRICS	DESIGN SIZES
Aida 11	12⅛" x 9⅛"
Aida 14	9½" x 7¼"
Hardanger 22	6" x 4⅝"

Anchor   **DMC (used for sample)**

Step 1: Cross-stitch (2 strands)

401	413 Pewter Gray-dk.

Step 2: Backstitch (1 strand)

401	413 Pewter Gray-dk.

MAY 1
May Day

May Day marks the middle of the Roman Floralia, or festival of Flora, the goddess of spring. In many countries, the day is also dedicated to people who work. This design combines both ideas: Flowers symbolize spring, and bees represent the industry of workers.

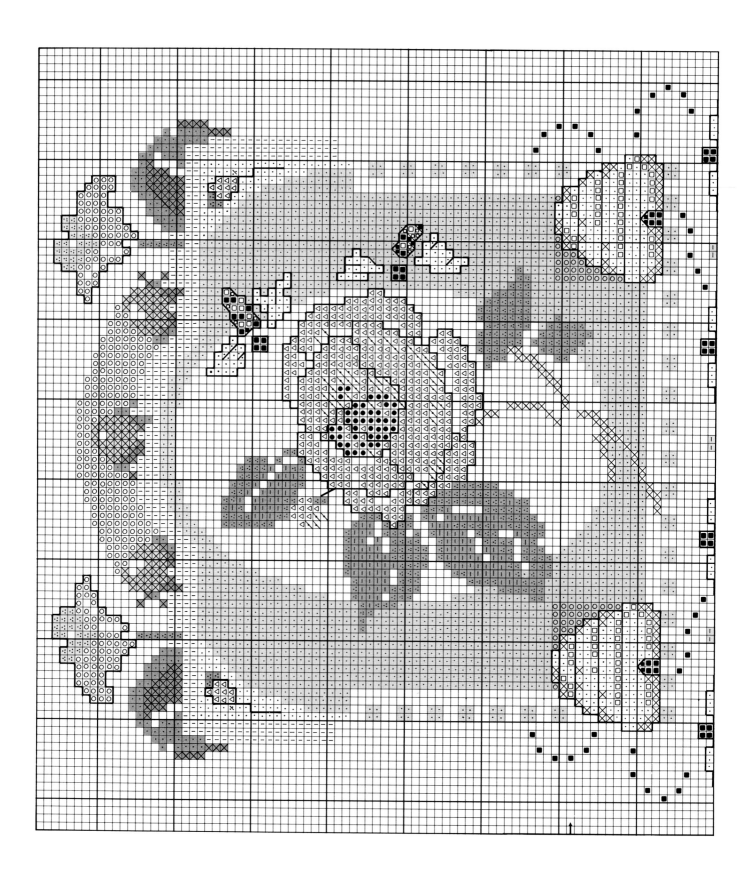

Stitch Count: 94 x 135

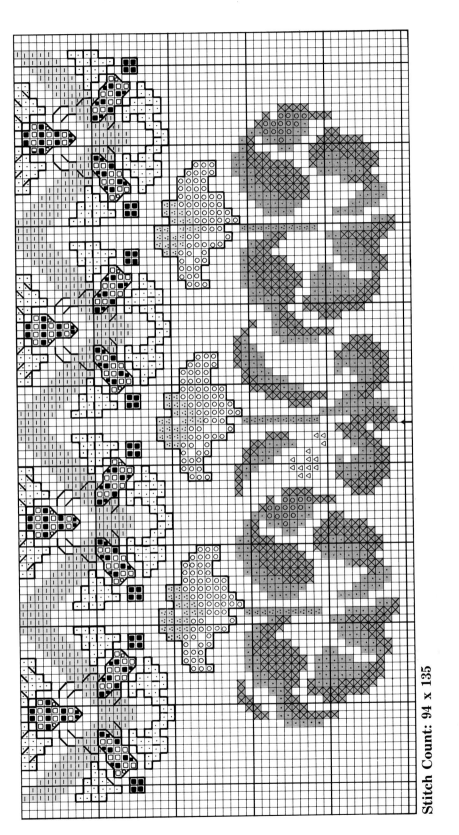

Busy Bees

SAMPLE
Stitched on Glenshee Egyptian
Cotton Quality D 28 over 2
threads, finished design size is 6¾"
x 9⅝". Fabric was cut 13" x 16".

FABRICS	**DESIGN SIZES**
Aida 11	8½" x 12¼"
Aida 14	6¾" x 9⅝"
Aida 18	5¼" x 7½"
Hardanger 22	4¼" x 6⅛"

Anchor			DMC (used for sample)	
	Step 1:		Cross-stitch (2 strands)	
292	·		3078	Golden Yellow-vy. lt.
301	□		744	Yellow-pale
9	○		760	Salmon
42	△		3350	Dusty Rose-vy. dk.
43	╱		815	Garnet-med.
72	●		902	Garnet-vy. dk.
158	·		828	Blue-ultra vy. lt.
167	○		519	Sky Blue
920	−		932	Antique Blue-lt.
117	⋮		341	Blue Violet-lt.
978	✕		322	Navy Blue-vy. lt.
208	○		563	Jade-lt.
208	−		563	Jade-lt. (1 strand)
210	✕		562	Jade-med.
189	✕		991	Aquamarine-dk.
215	▨		320	Pistachio Green-med.
246	✕		319	Pistachio Green-vy. dk.
362	✕		437	Tan-lt.
914	⋰		3064	Pecan-lt.
401	■		844	Beaver Gray-ultra dk.

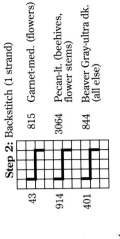

	Step 2:	Backstitch (1 strand)	
43		815	Garnet-med. (flowers)
914		3064	Pecan-lt. (beehives, flower stems)
401		844	Beaver Gray-ultra dk. (all else)

MAY 12
Mother's Day

This Mother's Day, don't just tell your mother how much you love her; show her by stitching this beautiful cutwork design. She'll be touched at the amount of time and care you put into its intricate detail. It's a Mother's Day keepsake that will remind her of your love for years.

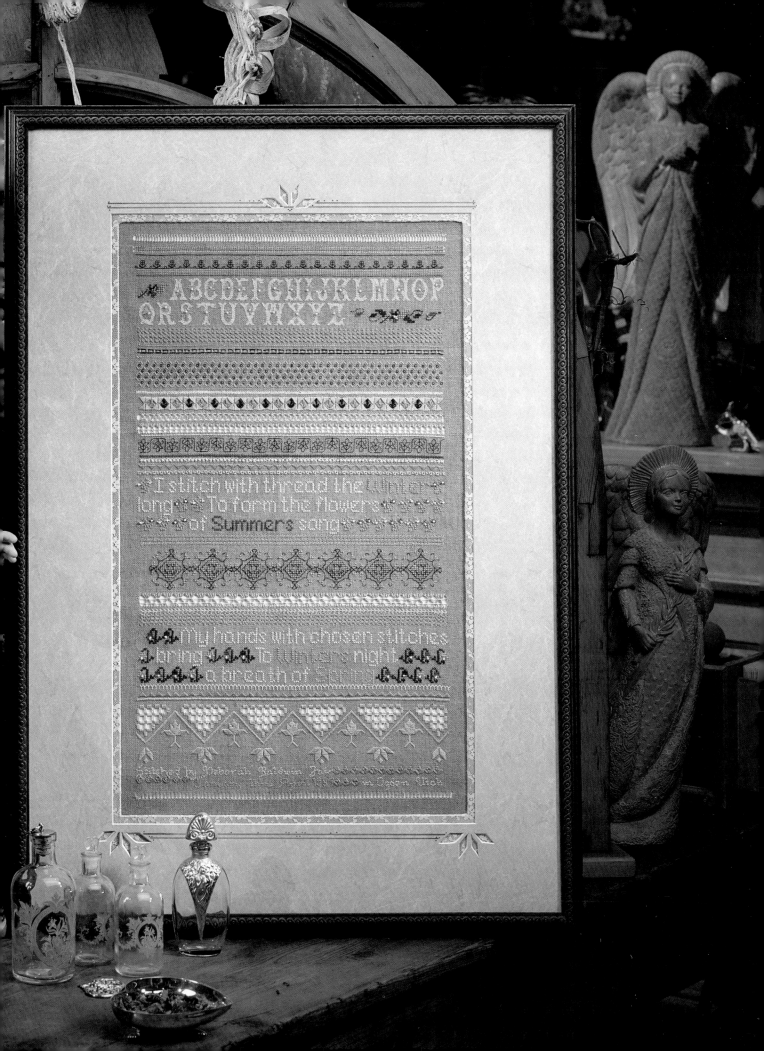

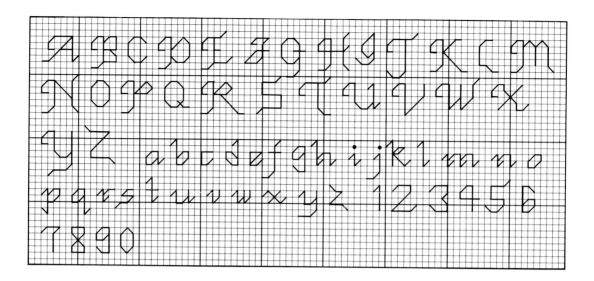

Mother's Day Sampler

SAMPLE

Stitched on raw Dublin linen 25, the finished design size is 13¼" x 23". The fabric was cut 20" x 30". Begin stitching Section 1 (3") from top and left edges. Work 1 section completely before proceeding to the next. Note that some sections are stitched over 1 thread. All others are stitched over 2 threads. The number of strands to be used, along with directions for each stitch, is indicated in parentheses following the color name. See General Instructions for specific stitches.

Additional materials needed:
DMC embroidery floss
225 Shell Pink-vy. lt.
224 Shell Pink-lt.
503 Blue Green-med.
500 Blue Green-vy. dk.
DMC Pearl Cotton
#12 Ecru
#8 Beige (color # 644)
Kreinik au ver a soie silk thread
4636A Burgundy
DMC Broder Medicis wool yarn
8408 Green-dk.

Belding buttonhole silk twist
5010 Beige
Ginnie Thompson flower thread
100 White
620 Mauve
Mill Hill glass beads
00123 Cream

Section 1: Ladder Hemstitch

Remove 6 horizontal threads. Hemstitch top and bottom edges in groups of 3 vertical threads.

Pearl Cotton #12-
Ecru (1 strand)

Section 2: Wrapped Backstitch

Remove 3 horizontal threads. Stitch in groups of 2 vertical threads on bottom edge of open area. Skip 2 horizontal threads. Remove 3 horizontal threads. Stitch in groups of 2 vertical threads on top edge of open area.

500 Blue Green-vy. dk. (1 strand)

Section 3: Backstitch

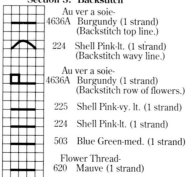

Au ver a soie-
4636A Burgundy (1 strand)
(Backstitch top line.)

224 Shell Pink-lt. (1 strand)
(Backstitch wavy line.)

Au ver a soie-
4636A Burgundy (1 strand)
(Backstitch row of flowers.)

225 Shell Pink-vy. lt. (1 strand)

224 Shell Pink-lt. (1 strand)

503 Blue Green-med. (1 strand)

Flower Thread-
620 Mauve (1 strand)

Section 4: Cross-stitch, Backstitch, Couching, French Knots, Beadwork

Cross-stitch letters over 1 thread with 1 strand of floss. All else is worked over 2 threads.

225 Shell Pink-vy. lt. (1 strand)

224 Shell Pink-lt. (1 strand)

Flower Thread-
620 Mauve (1 strand)

Au ver a soie-
4636A Burgundy (1 strand)

503 Blue Green-med. (2 strands)

Medicis Wool-
8408 Green-dk. (1 strand)

Medicis Wool-
8408 Green-dk. (1 strand)
(Backstitch)

Medicis Wool-
8408 Green-dk. (1 strand)
503 Blue Green-med. (1 strand)
(Couch the Medicis Wool with the floss.)

Buttonhole Twist-
5010 Beige (1 strand)
(French Knot, 1 wrap)

Beads-
00123 Cream
(Beadwork)

Section 5: Pulled Trellis Backstitch

Work over 4 vertical and 4 horizontal threads, pulling each stitch slightly.

503 Blue Green-med. (2 strands)

Section 6: Diagonal Stitch

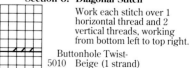

Work each stitch over 1 horizontal thread and 2 vertical threads, working from bottom left to top right.

Buttonhole Twist-
5010 Beige (1 strand)

Section 7: Threaded Running Stitch Variation

Buttonhole Twist-
5010 Beige (1 strand)

Au ver a soie-
4636A Burgundy (1 strand)

500 Blue Green-vy. dk. (2 strands)

Section 8: Diagonal Stitch

Repeat Section 6, reversing the direction of the stitch, working from bottom right to top left.

Buttonhole Twist-
5010 Beige (1 strand)

Section 9: Backstitch

Backstitch zigzag pattern over 4 horizontal and 4 vertical threads. Backstitch blocks over 2 horizontal and 2 vertical threads.

224 Shell Pink-lt. (2 strands)

500 Blue Green-vy. dk. (2 strands)

Section 10: Vandyke Stitch

Stitch over 3 horizontal and 2 vertical threads.

Flower Thread-
100 White (1 strand)

Section 11: Half Scotch Stitch, Lazy Daisy with Long Stitch, Bullion Stitch

Alternate direction of half Scotch stitches to form "window."

Pearl Cotton #8-
644 Beige (1 strand)

Stitch lazy daisy (leaves) and long stitch (stem) inside each "window," alternating light and dark colors.

503 Blue Green-med. (2 strands)

500 Blue Green-vy. dk. (2 strands)

Make 2 bullion stitches, crossed at the top, for each flower. Place a light pink flower over each light green stem and a burgundy flower over each dark green stem.

224 Shell Pink-lt. (2 strands)

Au ver a soie-
4636A Burgundy (1 strand)

Section 12: Serpentine Hemstitch

Remove 6 horizontal threads. Hemstitch top and bottom edges in groups of 4 vertical threads.

Pearl Cotton #12-
Ecru (1 strand)

Section 13: Twisted Ladder Hemstitch

Remove 8 horizontal threads. Hemstitch top and bottom edges in groups of 4 vertical threads, then work twist.

Pearl Cotton #12-
Ecru (1 strand)

Section 14: Couching with Cross-stitch

Couch flower thread with cross-stitches in pink floss.

Flower Thread-
100 White (1 strand)

224 Shell Pink-lt. (2 strands)

Section 15: Backstitch

500 Blue Green-vy. dk. (1 strand)

Section 16: Long-armed Cross-stitch

Stitch over 2 horizontal and 4 vertical threads.

Flower Thread-
620 Mauve (1 strand)

Section 17: Smyrna Cross-stitch

Flower Thread-
100 White (1 strand)

Section 18: Long Stitch

Each repeat is over 6 horizontal threads and 10 vertical threads.

503 Blue Green-med. (2 strands)

Section 19: Algerian Eye Stitch, Smyrna Cross-stitch

Alternate the 2 stitches, beginning with Algerian eye stitch and working over 4 vertical and 4 horizontal threads.

Buttonhole Twist-
5010 Beige (1 strand)

Section 20: Cross-stitch, Backstitch, Beadwork

Cross-stitch

225 Shell Pink-vy. lt. (2 strands)

224 Shell Pink-lt. (2 strands)

Flower Thread-
620 Mauve (1 strand)

Au ver a soie-
4636A Burgundy (1 strand)

503 Blue Green-med. (2 strands)

Medicis Wool-
8408 Green-dk. (1 strand)

503 Blue Green-med. (2 strands)
(Backstitch)

Beads-
00123 Cream
(Beadwork)

Section 21: Slanted Pulled Thread

Work over 4 vertical and 4 horizontal threads, pulling slightly to create small holes at dots.

224 Shell Pink-lt. (2 strands)

Section 22: Cross-stitch, Backstitch (Assisi work)

Cross-stitch

503 Blue Green-med. (2 strands)

Backstitch

Au ver a soie-
4636A Burgundy (1 strand)

Section 23: Double Twisted Hemstitch

Remove 12 horizontal threads. Hemstitch top and bottom edges in groups of 2 vertical threads, then work twists.

Pearl Cotton #12-
Ecru (1 strand)

Section 24: Fly Stitch

225 Shell Pink-vy. lt. (2 strands)

Section 25: Pulled Trellis Backstitch

Work over 4 vertical and 4 horizontal threads, pulling each stitch slightly.

224 Shell Pink-lt. (2 strands)

Section 26: Cross-stitch, Beadwork

Work from code for Section 20.

Section 27: Fly Stitch

Flower Thread-
100 White (1 strand)

Section 28: Long Stitch

Each repeat is over 4 horizontal threads and 6 vertical threads.

503 Blue Green-med. (2 strands)

Section 29: Satin Stitch

Each stitch is over 3 horizontal threads and 1 vertical thread.

Pearl Cotton #8-
644 Beige (1 strand)

Section 30: Hardanger Work

Kloster Blocks
Pearl Cotton #8-
644 Beige (1 strand)

Figure-8 wraps
Pearl Cotton #12-
Ecru (1 strand)

Section 31: Satin Stitch

Stitch over number of threads and in directions indicated on graph.

Pearl Cotton #8-
644 Beige (1 strand)

Section 32: Backstitch, Lazy Daisy, French Knots

225 Shell Pink-vy. lt. (2 strands)
(Backstitch name and place.)

224 Shell Pink-lt. (2 strands)
(Backstitch date.)

503 Blue Green-med. (2 strands)
(Stitch lazy daisy [leaves] and long stitch [stem].)

224 Shell Pink-lt. (1 strand)
(French Knots, 2 wraps)

Section 33: Basic Hemstitch

Remove 6 horizontal threads. Hemstitch in groups of 4 threads on bottom edge of open area.

Pearl Cotton #12-
Ecru (1 strand)

LADDER HEMSTITCH

WRAPPED BACKSTITCH

VANDYKE STITCH

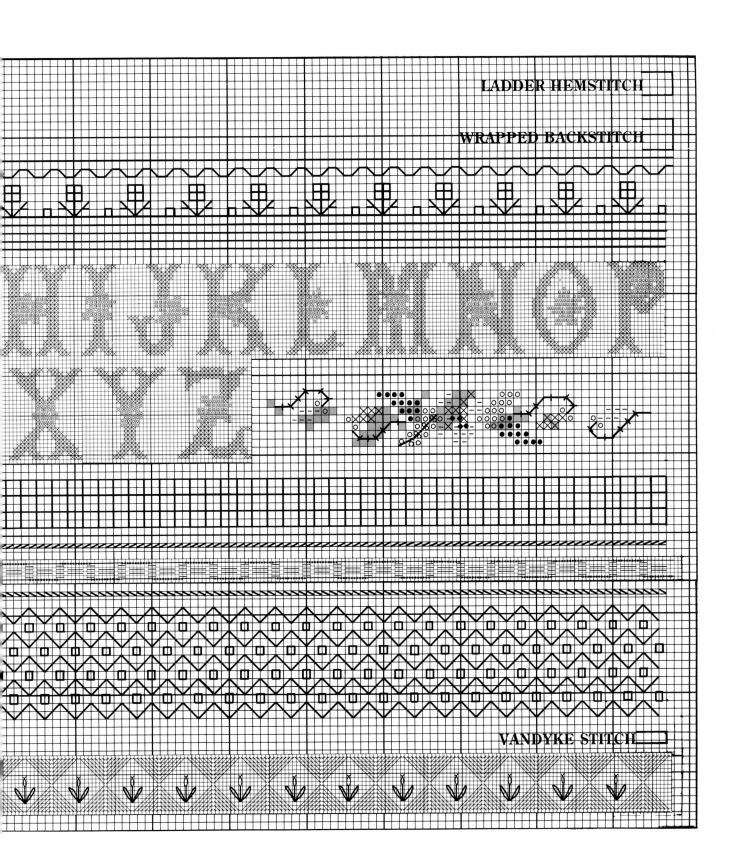

LADDER HEMSTITCH

WRAPPED BACKSTITCH

VANDYKE STITCH

59

SERPENTINE HEMSTITCH

TWISTED LADDER HEMSTITCH

LONG-ARMED CROSS-STITCH

BOTTOM PORTION

BASIC HEMSTITCH

BASIC HEMSTITCH

63

Bubbles and Balloons Festival

Carnival-colored balloons and iridescent bubbles floating through the air inspire a childlike awe and fascination. Re-create these simple pleasures by stitching this delightful gift bag to hold favors for your next patio party.

Festive Gift Bag

SAMPLE
Stitched on white Murano 30 over 2 threads, the finished design size is 8⅜″ x 5⅞″. The fabric was cut 12″ x 9″.

FABRICS	DESIGN SIZES
Aida 11	11⅜″ x 8″
Aida 14	8⅞″ x 6¼″
Aida 18	7″ x 4⅞″
Hardanger 22	5⅝″ x 4″

MATERIALS
Completed cross-stitch on white Murano 30; matching thread
¼ yard of unstitched white Murano 30
¼ yard of batting
¾ yard (45″-wide) blue fabric for lining and piping; matching thread
2½ yards of small cording
9½ yards (⅛″-wide) blue satin ribbon

DIRECTIONS
All seam allowances are ¼″.

1. With design centered, trim Murano to 10″ x 7½″. From unstitched white Murano, cut 1 (10″ x 7½″) piece for back, 2 (4½″ x 7½″) pieces for sides, and 1 (4½″ x 10″) piece for bottom. From blue fabric and batting, cut matching pieces for each Murano piece.

2. To make corded piping, cut a 1″-wide bias strip from blue fabric, piecing as needed to equal 2½ yards. Place cording in center of wrong side of bias strip and fold fabric over cording. Using a zipper foot, stitch close to cording through both layers of fabric. Trim seam allowance to ¼″. Cut 4 (7½″) lengths of piping for the sides of bag and 2 (29″) lengths for the top and bottom.

3. To make body of bag, pin batting pieces to wrong side of matching Murano pieces. Baste in place. With right sides facing and raw edges aligned, pin 1 (7½″) length of piping to left edge of design piece.

Stitch. Repeat with second 7½″ piece of piping and right edge of design piece. In the same manner, attach piping to left and right edges of back piece. With right sides facing and raw edges aligned, stitch design piece to 1 side piece, stitching on stitching line of piping. Repeat with second side piece and opposite edge of design piece. Stitch back to sides, stitching on stitching line of piping. Trim batting from seam allowances. Turn right side out.

4. With right sides facing and raw edges aligned, stitch 1 (29″) length of piping around top edge of bag body. Stitch remaining 29″ length of piping around bottom edge of bag body. Turn wrong side out. With right sides facing and corners of bottom matching side seams of bag body, stitch bottom to bag body, stitching on stitching line of piping. Trim batting from seam allowances. Clip corners. Turn right side out. Set aside.

5. With right sides facing and raw edges aligned, stitch lining pieces together as for bag, omitting piping and leaving a 3″ opening at 1 edge of bottom seam for turning. With right sides facing and side seams matching, slip Murano body into lining. Stitch bag and lining together around top edge, stitching on stitching line of piping. Turn bag through opening in lining. Slipstitch opening closed.

6. From ribbon, cut 8 (16″) lengths, 8 (18″) lengths, and 2 (32″) lengths. Handling 2 (16″) and 2 (18″) lengths of ribbon as 1, tie ribbon together to make a bow. Repeat to make 3 more bows. Knot

Stitch Count: 125 x 88

the 2 (32″) lengths together in the middle. Tack each raw end of ribbon to a corner of basket. Tack 1 bow to each corner of basket. If desired, attach balloons at knot in ribbons (see photograph).

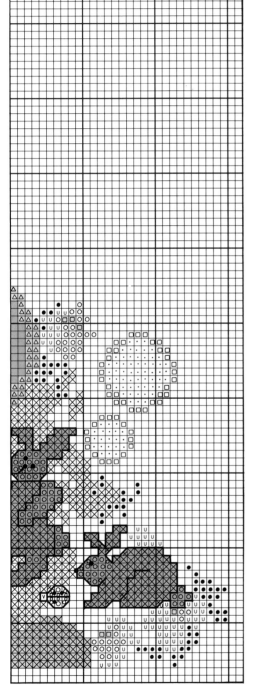

Anchor			DMC (used for sample)	
			Step 1: Cross-stitch (2 strands)	
387	–	/	712	Cream
387	+	+	712	Cream (2 strands) +
			014	Sky Blue Balger blending filament (1 strand)
300	G	6	745	Yellow-lt. pale
300		/	745	Yellow-lt. pale (1 strand)
306	▲	⌐	725	Topaz
306	△		725	Topaz (1 strand)
24	✕		776	Pink-med.
10	E		352	Coral-lt. (2 strands) +
			014	Sky Blue Balger blending filament (1 strand)
11	O	6	350	Coral-med.
47	□		321	Christmas Red
104	I	/	210	Lavender-med.
99	∴	⌐	552	Violet-dk.
158	·	/·	747	Sky Blue-vy. lt. (1 strand)
158	–	/	747	Sky Blue-vy. lt. (2 strands) +
			014	Sky Blue Balger blending filament (1 strand)
167	B		519	Sky Blue
167	H		519	Sky Blue (2 strands) +
			014	Sky Blue Balger blending filament (1 strand)
167	□		519	Sky Blue (1 strand)
128	S	⌐	775	Baby Blue-vy. lt.
159	O	6	3325	Baby Blue-lt.
130	∴	/	799	Delft-med.
121	△		793	Cornflower Blue-med. (2 strands) +
			014	Sky Blue Balger blending filament (1 strand)
940	■		792	Cornflower Blue-dk.
213	✕		369	Pistachio Green-vy. lt.
189	●		991	Aquamarine-dk.
324	U	4	922	Copper-lt.
362	O	6	437	Tan-lt.
309	✕	/	781	Topaz-dk.
898	□		611	Drab Brown-dk.
905	△	⌐	3031	Mocha Brown-vy. dk.
401	V		844	Beaver Gray-ultra dk.

Step 2: Backstitch (1 strand)

401		844	Beaver Gray-ultra dk.

Step 3: French Knots (1 strand)

401	●	844	Beaver Gray-ultra dk.

National Brides' Month

In the month of June, traditionally the popular month for weddings, thoughts turn to love—and brides. A bridal set, such as this one with lacy trim and intricate beadwork, will bring the sense of warmth to the occasion that only delicate handwork can.

Bridal Set

SAMPLE for Floral Mat

Stitched on white Aida 18, the finished design size is 6⅝" x 6⅝". The fabric was cut 13" x 13". Stitch only the floral border. See Suppliers for Mill Hill Beads.

SAMPLE for Ring Bearer's Pillow

Stitched on white Jobelan 28 over 2 threads, the finished design size is 8⅝" x 8⅝". Fabric was cut 12" x 12". See Suppliers for Mill Hill Beads.

Floral Mat and Ring Bearer's Pillow

FABRICS	DESIGN SIZES
Aida 11	10⅞" x 10⅞"
Aida 14	8⅝" x 8⅝"
Aida 18	6⅝" x 6⅝"
Hardanger 22	5½" x 5½"

SAMPLE for Table Square

Stitched on white Jobelan 28 over 2 threads, the finished design size is 2⅞" x 2⅞". The fabric was cut 19" x 19". The design was stitched on the corner of the fabric with the point of the heart 1¾" from left and bottom edges. See Suppliers for Mill Hill Beads.

SAMPLE for Handkerchief

Stitched on Waste Canvas 14, the finished design size is 2⅞" x 2⅞". The canvas was cut 5" x 5". The design was stitched on the corner of a purchased linen handkerchief with the point of the heart 1" from left and bottom edges. See Suppliers for Mill Hill Beads.

Table Square and Handkerchief

FABRICS	DESIGN SIZES
Aida 11	3⅝" x 3¾"
Aida 14	2⅞" x 2⅞"
Aida 18	2¼" x 2¼"
Hardanger 22	1⅞" x 1⅞"

MATERIALS for Floral Mat

Completed cross-stitch on white Aida 18
Professionally cut mat (see Step 1 below)
Double-sided tape
Masking tape
Dressmakers' pen

DIRECTIONS

1. Have a professional framer cut the mat board. The outside dimensions should be 7½" x 7½". For the window, a 5⅛"-diameter circle should be cut.

2. With design centered, trim the Aida to measure 9½" x 9½".

3. Place the Aida wrong side up on a flat surface. Center the mat on the fabric and, with dressmakers' pen, trace the edge of the window onto the fabric. Then draw a smaller window 2" inside the first window. Cut along inside pen line. Clip the material between the 2 pen lines at ⅜" intervals.

4. On the wrong side of the mat, run a strip of double-sided tape around the edge of the window and around outside edge of mat. Fold the fabric over the mat edges, pulling it taut to fit. Secure with masking tape.

5. Place the mat in a ready-made frame or have a professional framer complete the framing.

MATERIALS for Ring Bearer's Pillow

Completed cross-stitch on white Jobelan 28
8¾" square of white satin
1¼ yards (3½"-wide) white bridal lace
1⅓ yards (⅛"-wide) white satin ribbon
Approximately 2,000 lavender glass beads
Polyester stuffing
Beading needle
White thread

DIRECTIONS

All seam allowances are ¼".

1. With design centered, trim Jobelan to 8¾" square. With right sides facing and raw edges aligned, stitch design piece to satin square, leaving an opening on 1 side for turning. Turn right side out. Stuff firmly. Slipstitch opening closed.

2. Following pattern in lace, tack beads to lace as desired (see photo).

3. Slipstitch straight edge of lace to edges of pillow, pleating lace at each corner to fit.

4. Cut 2 (23") lengths of satin ribbon. Fold each length in half. Tack 1 ribbon fold to Jobelan 1" below tip of 1 beaded heart (see photo) on previous page. Tack remaining ribbon below opposite heart in same manner. Tie each ribbon in a small bow, leaving long tails.

MATERIALS for Table Square
Completed cross-stitch on white
  Jobelan 28
2 yards (2½"-wide) white bridal
  lace
Approximately 1,000 lavender
  glass beads
Beading needle
White thread

DIRECTIONS
  1. Fold edges of Jobelan under ¼"
twice. Slipstitch hem in place.

  2. Following pattern in lace, tack
beads to lace as desired (see
photo).

  3. Slipstitch straight edge of lace
to edges of table square, pleating
lace at each corner to fit.

MATERIALS for Handkerchief
Completed cross-stitch on 9½"-
  square white handkerchief
1½ yards (1½"-wide) white bridal
  lace

Approximately 250 lavender
  glass beads
Beading needle
White thread

DIRECTIONS
  1. Following pattern in lace, tack
beads to lace as desired (see
photo).

  2. Slipstitch straight edge of lace
to edge of handkerchief, pleating
lace at each corner to fit.

Stitch Count: 120 x 120

72

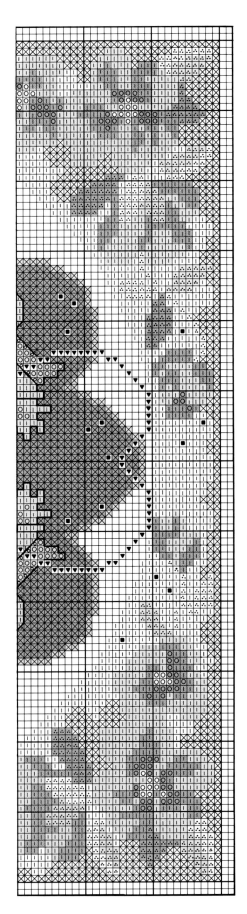

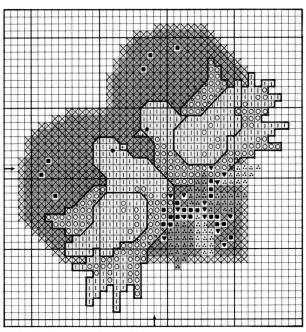

Stitch Count: 40 x 41

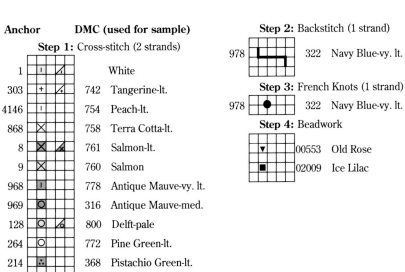

Anchor			DMC (used for sample)	
			Step 1: Cross-stitch (2 strands)	
1	I	⧄		White
303	+	⧄	742	Tangerine-lt.
4146	I		754	Peach-lt.
868	✕		758	Terra Cotta-lt.
8	✕	⧄	761	Salmon-lt.
9	✕		760	Salmon
968	I		778	Antique Mauve-vy. lt.
969	○		316	Antique Mauve-med.
128	○	⧄	800	Delft-pale
264	○		772	Pine Green-lt.
214	∴		368	Pistachio Green-lt.
875	∴		503	Blue Green-med.
876	∴		502	Blue Green

Step 2: Backstitch (1 strand)

978		322	Navy Blue-vy. lt.

Step 3: French Knots (1 strand)

978	●	322	Navy Blue-vy. lt.

Step 4: Beadwork

▼	00553	Old Rose
■	02009	Ice Lilac

JUNE 14
Flag Day

"Resolved, That the flag of the thirteen United States shall be thirteen stripes, alternate red and white; that the union be thirteen stars, white on a field of blue, representing a new constellation." On June 14, 1777, John Adams introduced this resolution to the Continental Congress in Philadelphia. Since that day, the constellation has grown bigger and brighter. Unfurl your flag and honor the freedom that it represents.

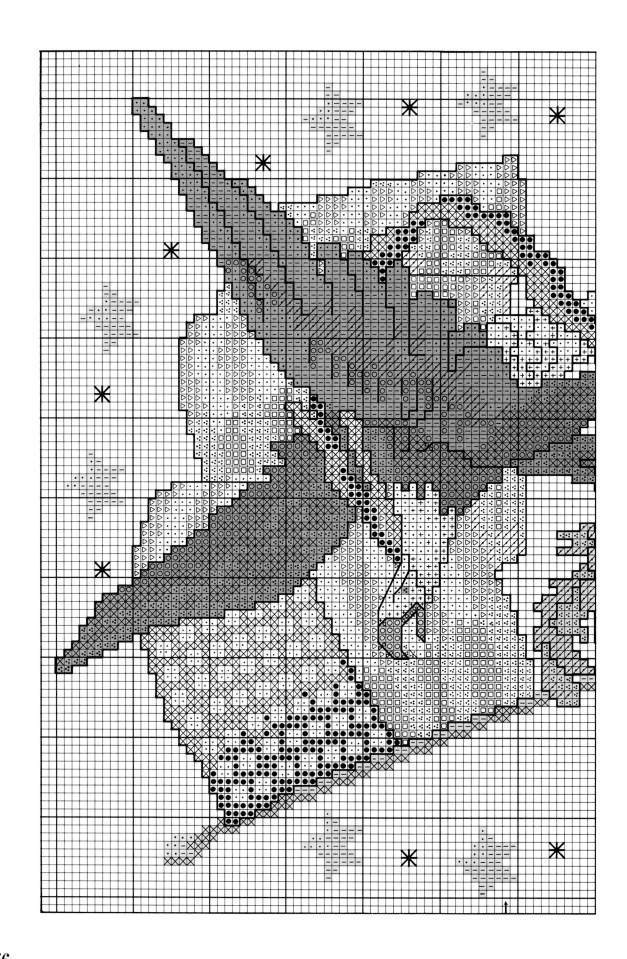

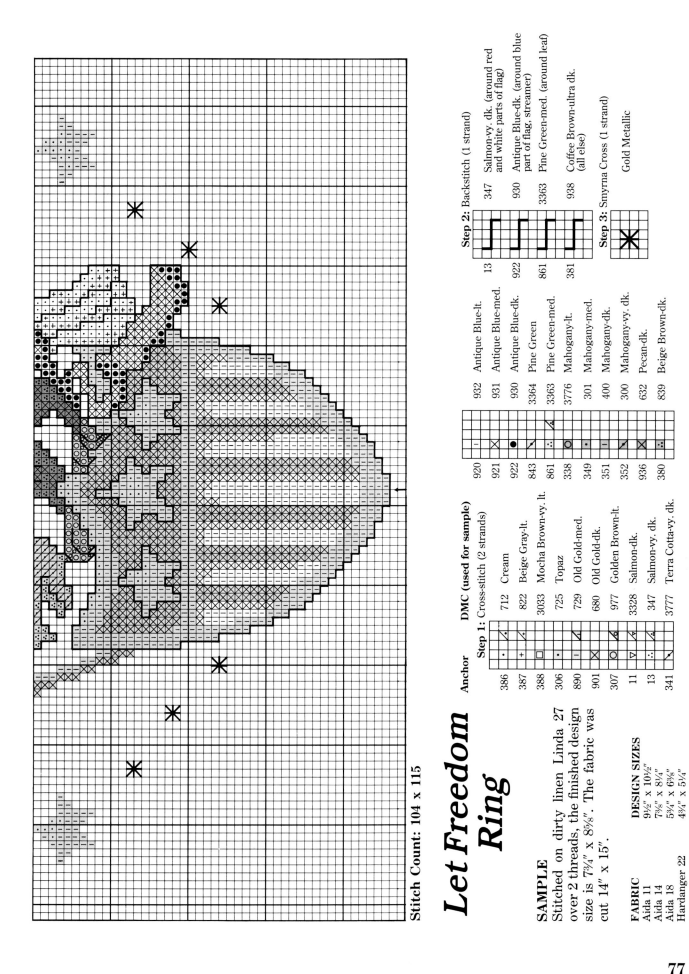

Let Freedom Ring

SAMPLE

Stitched on dirty linen Linda 27 over 2 threads, the finished design size is 7¾" x 8⅝". The fabric was cut 14" x 15".

FABRIC	DESIGN SIZES
Aida 11	9½" x 10½"
Aida 14	7⅜" x 8¼"
Aida 18	5¾" x 6⅜"
Hardanger 22	4¾" x 5¼"

Anchor   **DMC (used for sample)**

Step 1: Cross-stitch (2 strands)

		Anchor	DMC	
·		386	712	Cream
+		387	822	Beige Gray-lt.
□		388	3033	Mocha Brown-vy. lt.
·		306	725	Topaz
−		890	729	Old Gold-med.
⊠		901	680	Old Gold-dk.
○		307	977	Golden Brown-lt.
▽		11	3328	Salmon-dk.
∴		13	347	Salmon-vy. dk.
◸		341	3777	Terra Cotta-vy. dk.

		Anchor	DMC	
−		920	932	Antique Blue-lt.
⊠		921	931	Antique Blue-med.
●		922	930	Antique Blue-dk.
◿		843	3364	Pine Green
∴		861	3363	Pine Green-med.
○		338	3776	Mahogany-lt.
·		349	301	Mahogany-med.
−		351	400	Mahogany-vy. dk.
◿		352	300	Mahogany-vy. dk.
⊠		936	632	Pecan-dk.
⋅⋅		380	839	Beige Brown-dk.

Step 2: Backstitch (1 strand)

	347	Salmon-vy. dk. (around red and white parts of flag)
	930	Antique Blue-dk. (around blue part of flag, streamer)
	3363	Pine Green-med. (around leaf)
	938	Coffee Brown-ultra dk. (all else)

	13
	922
	861
	381

Step 3: Smyrna Cross (1 strand)

✳	Gold Metallic

JUNE 16
Father's Day

Show your dad he holds a soft spot in your heart with these decorative pillows. The rustic theme, combined with an elegant touch of satin, is sure to please.

Wildlife Pillow Set

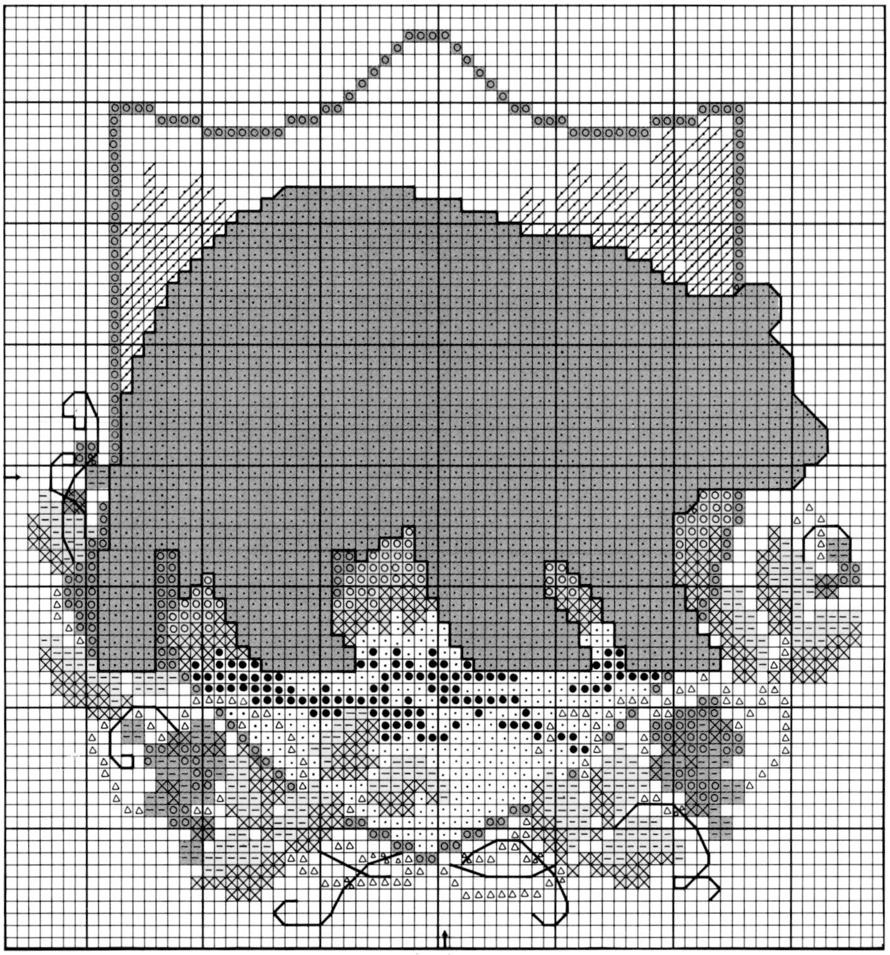

Stitch Count: 71 x 74

SAMPLE for Bear
Stitched on pewter Murano 30 over 2 threads, the finished design size is 4¾" x 4⅞". The fabric was cut 11" x 11".

FABRICS	DESIGN SIZES
Aida 11	6½" x 6¾"
Aida 14	5⅛" x 5¼"
Aida 18	4" x 4⅛"
Hardanger 22	3¼" x 3⅜"

SAMPLE for Mountain Lion
Stitched on pewter Murano 30 over 2 threads, the finished design size is 5½" x 5". The fabric was cut 12" x 11".

FABRICS	DESIGN SIZES
Aida 11	7½" x 6⅞"
Aida 14	5⅞" x 5⅜"
Aida 18	4½" x 4⅛"
Hardanger 22	3¾" x 3⅜"

MATERIALS (for 1 pillow)
Completed cross-stitch on pewter Murano 30
¾ yard (45"-wide) burgundy satin; matching thread
½ yard (45"-wide) green polyester lining fabric
2¾ yards of medium cording
14"-square box pillow form

DIRECTIONS
All seam allowances are ¼".

1. With design centered, trim the Murano to a 7" square. From satin, cut 4 (3¼" x 13") pieces for border, 1 (12½"-square) piece for back, and 1 (50" x 2") boxing strip. From the lining fabric, cut 1"-wide bias strips, piecing as needed to make 2¾ yards.

2. To make corded piping, place cording in center of wrong side of bias strip and fold fabric over it. Using a zipper foot, stitch close to cording through both layers of fabric. Trim seam allowance to ¼".

3. To attach border strip to design piece, mark center of 1 long edge of each border strip and the center of each edge of design piece. With right sides facing, centers matching, and raw edges aligned, stitch border strips to design piece. Stitch to within ¼" of each corner; backstitch. Repeat to attach all border strips. Press seams toward border.

4. To miter corners of border, fold right sides of 2 adjacent border strips together and stitch at 45° angle (see Diagram). Repeat for each corner. Trim to ¼".

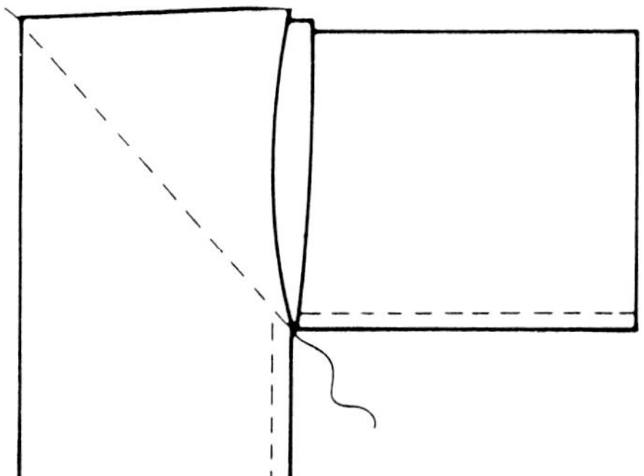

Diagram

5. To attach piping, with right sides facing and raw edges aligned, stitch piping to pillow front on

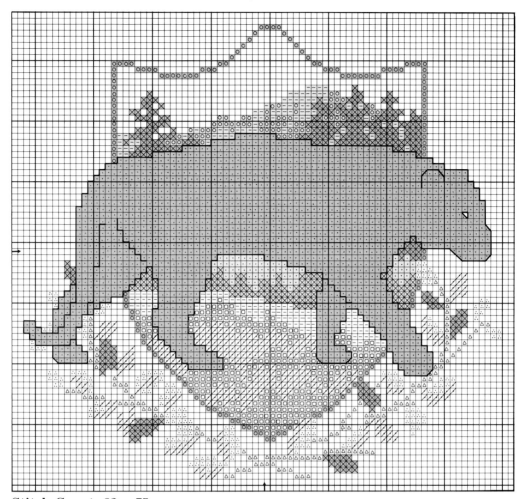

Stitch Count: 82 x 75

stitching line of piping. Repeat for pillow back.

6. With right sides facing and raw edges aligned, pin boxing strip to pillow front. Begin stitching 1″ from 1 end of boxing strip and continue around entire edge of pillow front. Then stitch ends of boxing strip together at a 45° angle. Trim to ¼″.

7. With right sides facing and raw edges aligned, stitch boxing strip to pillow back, leaving 1 side open. Turn right side out. Insert pillow form. Slipstitch opening closed.

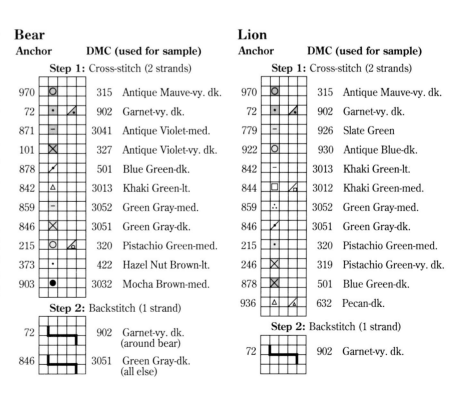

Bear

Anchor		DMC (used for sample)	
		Step 1: Cross-stitch (2 strands)	
970		315	Antique Mauve-vy. dk.
72		902	Garnet-vy. dk.
871		3041	Antique Violet-med.
101		327	Antique Violet-vy. dk.
878		501	Blue Green-dk.
842		3013	Khaki Green-lt.
859		3052	Green Gray-med.
846		3051	Green Gray-dk.
215		320	Pistachio Green-med.
373		422	Hazel Nut Brown-lt.
903		3032	Mocha Brown-med.
		Step 2: Backstitch (1 strand)	
72		902	Garnet-vy. dk. (around bear)
846		3051	Green Gray-dk. (all else)

Lion

Anchor		DMC (used for sample)	
		Step 1: Cross-stitch (2 strands)	
970		315	Antique Mauve-vy. dk.
72		902	Garnet-vy. dk.
779		926	Slate Green
922		930	Antique Blue-dk.
842		3013	Khaki Green-lt.
844		3012	Khaki Green-med.
859		3052	Green Gray-med.
846		3051	Green Gray-dk.
215		320	Pistachio Green-med.
246		319	Pistachio Green-vy. dk.
878		501	Blue Green-dk.
936		632	Pecan-dk.
		Step 2: Backstitch (1 strand)	
72		902	Garnet-vy. dk.

81

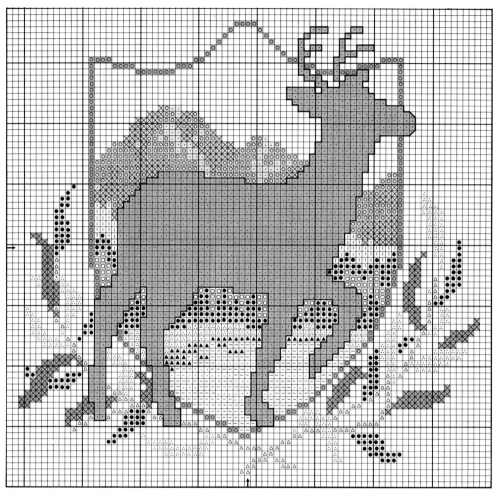

Stitch Count: 79 x 75

SAMPLE for Deer
Stitched on pewter Murano 30 over 2 threads, the finished design size is 5¼" x 5". The fabric was cut 12" x 11".

FABRICS	DESIGN SIZES
Aida 11	7⅛" x 6⅞"
Aida 14	5⅝" x 5⅜"
Aida 18	4⅜" x 4⅛"
Hardanger 22	3⅝" x 3⅜"

Deer

Anchor		DMC (used for sample)

Step 1: Cross-stitch (2 strands)

926	·		Ecru
970	O		315	Antique Mauve-vy. dk.
72	·	╱	902	Garnet-vy. dk.
920	−		932	Antique Blue-lt.

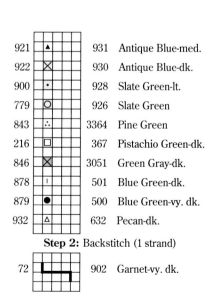

921	▲	931	Antique Blue-med.
922	✕	930	Antique Blue-dk.
900	·	928	Slate Green-lt.
779	O	926	Slate Green
843	∴	3364	Pine Green
216	☐	367	Pistachio Green-dk.
846	✕	3051	Green Gray-dk.
878	ı	501	Blue Green-dk.
879	●	500	Blue Green-vy. dk.
932	△	632	Pecan-dk.

Step 2: Backstitch (1 strand)

72	⌐	902	Garnet-vy. dk.

82

Red, White, and Boom Day

In Columbus, Ohio, the townspeople get a head start on Independence Day by beginning the celebration on July 3rd with one of the largest fireworks displays in the Midwest. You can start celebrating early, too, with a family gathering or neighborhood barbecue. Show your colors and be chef of the day in this red, white, and blue apron with patriotic motifs.

All-American Apron

SAMPLE

All designs are stitched on a purchased butcher apron using Waste Canvas 10. Center *July 4* horizontally, placing the *J* 2" below the top edge of the apron bib. Place remaining designs as desired on apron (see photo).

MOTIF	FINISHED DESIGN SIZES
July 4th	7⅛" x 4½"
Let Freedom Ring	15¼" x 1¾"
Give Me Liberty	8½" x 3"
In God We Trust	5½" x 3½"
America the Beautiful	11¼" x 3½"

MOTIF	CANVAS SIZES
July 4th	10" x 7"
Let Freedom Ring	18" x 4"
Give Me Liberty	11" x 5"
In God We Trust	8" x 6"
America the Beautiful	14" x 6"

Step 1: Cross-stitch (1 strand of Pearl Cotton #5)

Anchor Pearl Cotton		DMC Pearl Cotton #5 (used for sample)	
1	·		White
47	○	321	Christmas Red
132	●	797	Royal Blue
400	✕	414	Steel Gray-dk.

Stitch Count: 55 x 35

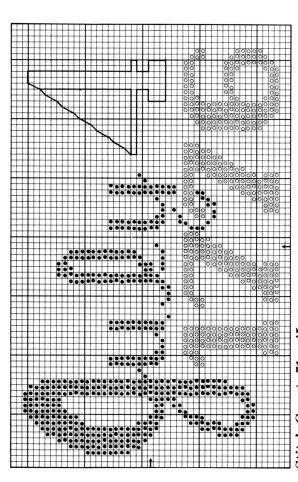

Stitch Count: 71 x 45

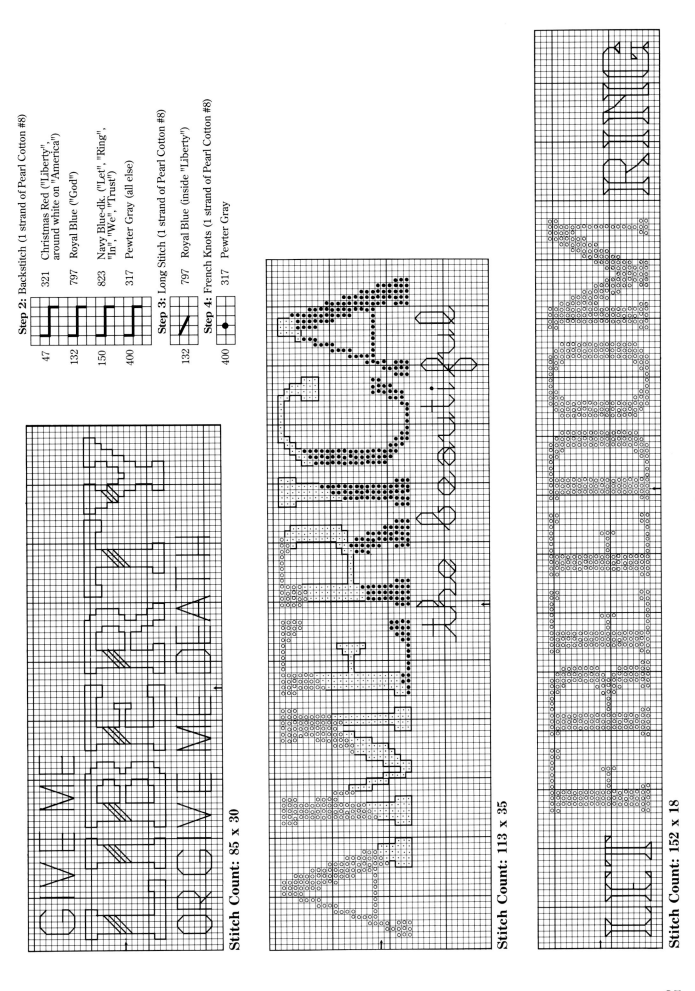

Stitch Count: 85 x 30

Stitch Count: 113 x 35

Stitch Count: 152 x 18

Watermelon Festival

Everyone enjoys a cool, juicy watermelon on a hot summer day. But in Mize, Mississippi, they don't just enjoy it, they have a festival to honor it. You, too, can commemorate the watermelon season with these seed packets decorated with a cross-stitched melon eater and watermelon buttons.

Seed Packets

SAMPLE
Stitched on white Aida 14, the finished design size is 3⅜″ x 4¾″. The fabric was cut 11″ x 12″.

FABRICS	DESIGN SIZES
Aida 11	4¼″ x 6⅛″
Aida 18	2⅝″ x 3¾″
Hardanger 22	2⅛″ x 3″

MATERIALS (for 1 packet)
Completed cross-stitch design on
  white Aida 14; matching thread
¼ yard of white fabric for lining
⅓ yard (1/16″-wide) pink or blue
  satin braid
2 watermelon buttons
Large-eyed needle
Dressmakers' pen

DIRECTIONS
All seam allowances are ¼″.

1. Enlarge pattern for seed packet. Place pattern over design piece, centering design horizontally within fold lines and with bottom edge of design ¾″ from bottom of fabric. Cut out. From white fabric, cut a matching piece for lining.

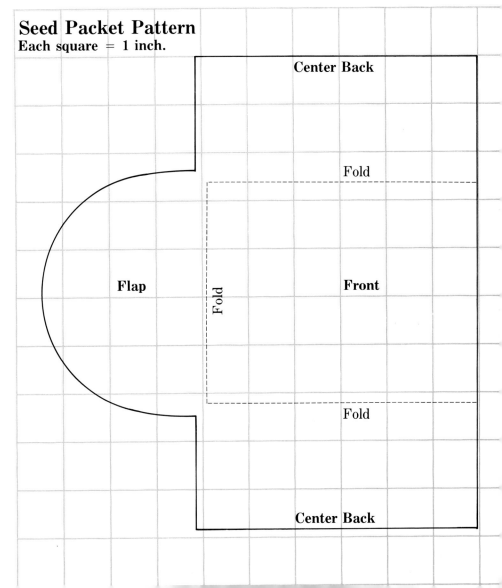

Seed Packet Pattern
Each square = 1 inch.

Center Back

Fold

Flap

Fold

Front

Fold

Center Back

2. With right sides facing, stitch 6″ edges together to form center back seam. Trim seam allowance to ⅛″. Fold fabric along fold lines at sides and stitch across bottom through all layers. Trim seam allowance to ⅛″. Turn. Repeat to stitch lining, leaving a small opening in bottom seam for turning. Do not turn.

3. With right sides facing, slide lining over design piece. With raw edges aligned, stitch around top edge of packet, including flap. Turn through opening in lining. Slipstitch opening closed. Tuck lining into packet.

4. To attach buttons, mark center of flap 1″ from bottom edge. Close flap and mark ¾″ below flap edge directly opposite first mark. Sew 1 button at each mark.

5. To attach braid to flap, thread needle with braid; knot 1 end. Insert needle on wrong side of flap directly under button. Bring needle and braid up through both layers. To close flap, wrap ribbon in a figure-8 pattern around the buttons.

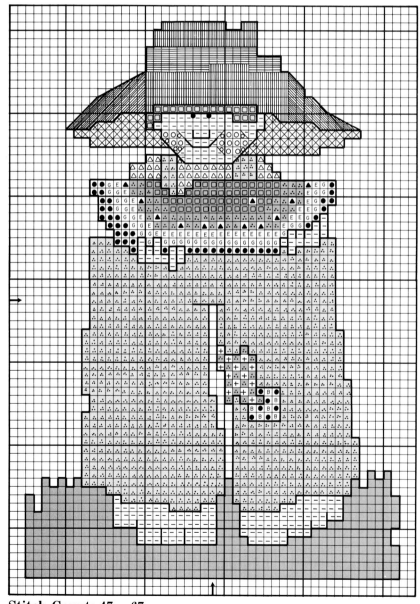

Stitch Count: 47 x 67

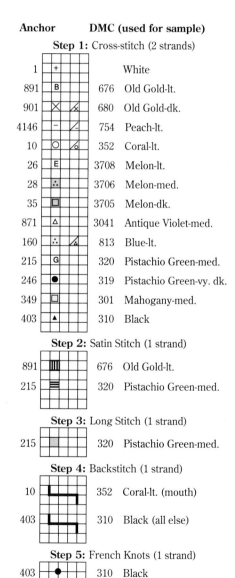

Anchor		DMC (used for sample)	
Step 1: Cross-stitch (2 strands)			
1	+		White
891	B	676	Old Gold-lt.
901	X ⤢	680	Old Gold-dk.
4146	− ⤢	754	Peach-lt.
10	O ⤢	352	Coral-lt.
26	E	3708	Melon-lt.
28	∴	3706	Melon-med.
35	□	3705	Melon-dk.
871	△	3041	Antique Violet-med.
160	∴ ⤢	813	Blue-lt.
215	G	320	Pistachio Green-med.
246	●	319	Pistachio Green-vy. dk.
349	□	301	Mahogany-med.
403	▲	310	Black
Step 2: Satin Stitch (1 strand)			
891	▥	676	Old Gold-lt.
215	▤	320	Pistachio Green-med.
Step 3: Long Stitch (1 strand)			
215	▨	320	Pistachio Green-med.
Step 4: Backstitch (1 strand)			
10	⌐	352	Coral-lt. (mouth)
403	⌐	310	Black (all else)
Step 5: French Knots (1 strand)			
403	●	310	Black

JULY 24
Rodeo Day

In 1847, Brigham Young led a wagon train of Mormon pioneers into the Salt Lake Valley of Utah. The occasion is now celebrated by residents of Utah annually as a state holiday, with parades, rodeos, picnics, and other festivities. Here a pint-sized cowboy in a 10-gallon hat and boots captures the fun of this festive day.

Ride 'Em, Cowboy

SAMPLE

Stitched on Rustico 14, finished design size is 3″ x 4¼″. Fabric was cut 7″ x 12″.

FABRICS	DESIGN SIZES
Aida 11	3⅞″ x 5½″
Aida 14	3″ x 4¼″
Aida 18	2⅜″ x 3⅜″
Hardanger 22	1⅞″ x 2¾″

Anchor		DMC (used for sample)	
Step 1: Cross-stitch (2 strands)			
926		Ecru	
891		676	Old Gold-lt.
4146		754	Peach-lt.
11		3328	Salmon-dk.
13		347	Salmon-vy. dk.
164		824	Blue-vy. dk.
307		977	Golden Brown-lt.
362		437	Tan-lt.
309		435	Brown-vy. lt.
371		433	Brown-med.
8581		646	Beaver Gray-dk.

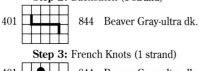

Step 2: Backstitch (1 strand)

401		844	Beaver Gray-ultra dk.

Step 3: French Knots (1 strand)

401		844	Beaver Gray-ultra dk.

Step 4: Long Loose Stitch (1 strand)

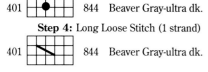

401		844	Beaver Gray-ultra dk.

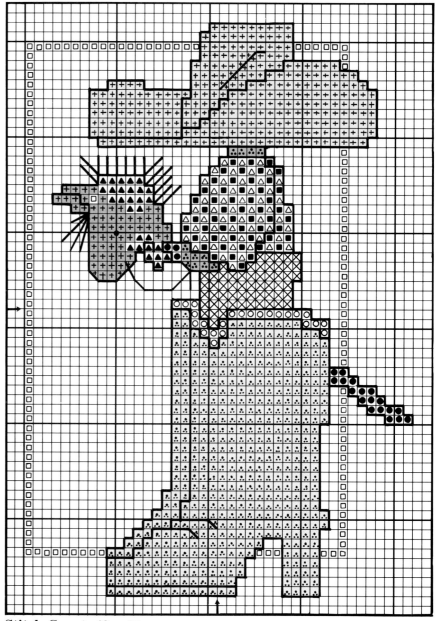

Stitch Count: 42 x 60

AUGUST 28
Herb Day

Herb Day originated in 1980 at the Duke Homestead in North Carolina. Its purpose was to educate visitors on the role herbs played in rural life during the 19th century. Herbs are pretty, too, as you can see from this kitchen set.

Kitchen Set

SAMPLES

Stitched on ivory Linda 27 over 2 threads, finished design size is 4¼″ x 4¼″ for each design. Fabric was cut 9″ x 9″ for each design.

FABRICS	DESIGN SIZES
Aida 11	5¼″ x 5¼″
Aida 14	4⅛″ x 4⅛″
Aida 18	3¼″ x 3¼″
Hardanger 22	2⅝″ x 2⅝″

MATERIALS (for canister cover)

Completed cross-stitch on ivory Linda 27
¼ yard of unstitched ivory Linda 27; matching thread
½ yard (45″-wide) purple print fabric; matching thread
1 (22″) square of fleece
1½ yards of small cording
1 (3-pound-size) can

DIRECTIONS

All seam allowances are ¼″.

1. With design centered, trim design piece to 5½″ square. From unstitched Linda, cut 1 (8½″ x 21″) piece for top section, 1 (5½″ x 16″) piece for side section, 1 (1½″ x 21″) piece for bottom strip, and 1 (7″-diameter) circle for bottom. From purple fabric, cut 1 (14½″ x 21″) piece and 1 (7″-diameter) bottom circle for lining; also cut 1″-wide bias strips, piecing as needed to equal 54″. Set aside remaining fabric. To make 54″ of corded piping, place cording in center on wrong side of bias strip and fold fabric over it. Stitch close to cording. From piping, cut 2 (21″) pieces and 2 (5½″) pieces. From fleece, cut 1 (14½″ x 21″) piece and 1 (7″-diameter) bottom circle.

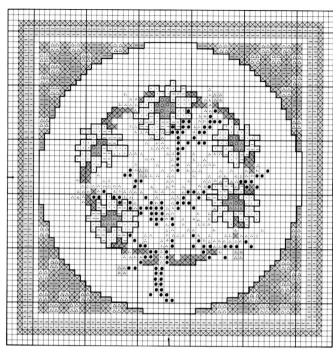

Stitch Count: 58 x 58 (for each design)
Chamomile

2. To attach piping, with right sides facing and raw edges aligned, stitch 1 (5½″) piece to each side of design piece. Then, with right sides facing, raw edges aligned, and piping sandwiched between, stitch 1 end of side section to 1 side of design piece, sewing on stitching line of piping. Repeat on other side to make a tube.

3. With right sides facing and raw edges aligned, stitch 1 (21″) piece of piping to 1 long edge of bottom strip, sewing on stitching line of piping. Stitch ends of bottom strip together to form a tube. With right sides facing and piping sandwiched between, stitch bottom tube to bottom of design tube, placing seam in back.

4. To attach bottom, with right sides facing, stitch 7″-diameter Linda circle to bottom tube. Clip curves and turn.

5. With right sides facing, stitch remaining piece of piping to 1 edge of 8½″ x 21″ top section, sewing on stitching line. With right

sides facing, stitch ends of top section together to make a tube. With right sides facing and piping side toward design tube, stitch top section tube to design tube, aligning seam in back with bottom tube seam. Set aside.

6. To make lining, pin fleece to wrong sides of matching lining pieces. With right sides facing, stitch 14½″ ends of lining piece together to form a tube, leaving an opening for turning. With right sides facing and raw edges aligned, stitch lining circle to lining piece. Do not turn. With right sides facing, slide lining over cover. Stitch together around top edge. Turn through opening in lining. Slipstitch opening closed. Tuck lining inside cover.

7. To make tie, cut and piece ½″-wide strips from remaining purple fabric to equal 43″. Fold long edges under ⅛″ and press. With wrong sides facing, fold strip in half lengthwise. Edgestitch. Knot ends. Place can inside cover. Tie the tie in a bow around cover.

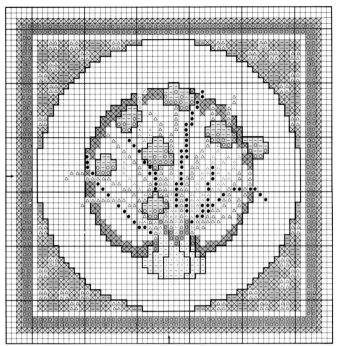

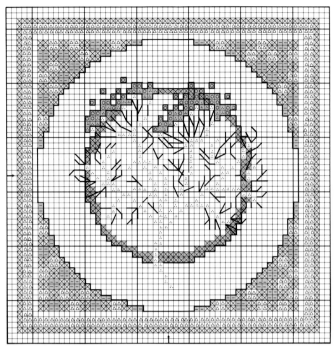

Chives

Dill

MATERIALS (for dish towel)
Completed cross-stitch on ivory
Linda 27
½ yard of unstitched ivory Linda
27; matching thread
¼ yard (45″-wide) purple print
fabric; matching thread
1¼ yards of small cording

DIRECTIONS
All seam allowances are ¼″.

1. With design centered, trim
Linda to 5½″ square. From unstitched Linda, cut 1 (17″ x 17½″)
piece for towel, 2 (6½″ x 5½″)
pieces for side sections, and 1 (4½″
x 17″) strip for bottom border.
From purple fabric, cut 1″-wide
bias strips, piecing as needed to
equal 45″. To make 45″ of corded
piping, place cording in center of
wrong side of bias strip and fold
fabric over it. Using a zipper foot,
stitch close to cording through
both layers of fabric. Cut 2 (17″)
and 2 (5½″) pieces of piping.

2. To attach piping, with right
sides facing, stitch 1 (5½″) piece of

piping to each side of design piece.
With right sides facing and piping
sandwiched between, stitch 1 side
of design piece to 1 end of 1 side
section, sewing on stitching line of
piping. Repeat on other side with
remaining side section.

3. With right sides facing and
raw edges aligned, stitch 1 remaining piece of piping to 1 (17″) edge of
towel piece. Repeat on 1 (17″) edge
of bottom border piece. With right
sides facing and piping sandwiched
between, stitch towel piece to top
of design piece, sewing on stitching line of piping. In same manner,
stitch bottom border to bottom of
design piece.

4. To hem bottom of towel piece,
fold raw edge of bottom border
under ¼″. Fold to back of towel for
doubled hem. Slipstitch hem in
place, covering raw edges of the
piping.

5. To finish side and top edges of
towel, fold raw edges under ¼″
twice. Slipstitch in place, mitering
top corners. Press towel.

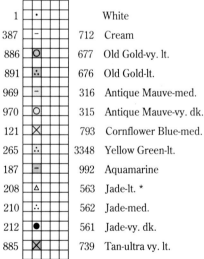

Anchor		DMC (used for sample)	
Step 1: Cross-stitch (2 strands)			
1	•		White
387	–	712	Cream
886	O	677	Old Gold-vy. lt.
891	∴	676	Old Gold-lt.
969	–	316	Antique Mauve-med.
970	O	315	Antique Mauve-vy. dk.
121	X	793	Cornflower Blue-med.
265	∴	3348	Yellow Green-lt.
187	–	992	Aquamarine
208	△	563	Jade-lt. *
210	∴	562	Jade-med.
212	●	561	Jade-vy. dk.
885	X	739	Tan-ultra vy. lt.

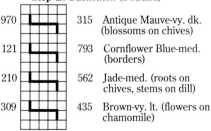

Step 2: Backstitch (1 strand)			
970		315	Antique Mauve-vy. dk. (blossoms on chives)
121		793	Cornflower Blue-med. (borders)
210		562	Jade-med. (roots on chives, stems on dill)
309		435	Brown-vy. lt. (flowers on chamomile)

* On towel, 316 DMC was used instead of
563 DMC.

Music Theater Festival

Throughout the summer, there are festivals all across the country for every kind of music, from bluegrass to blues. In September, we celebrate the culmination of these events with a jazz band in silhouette.

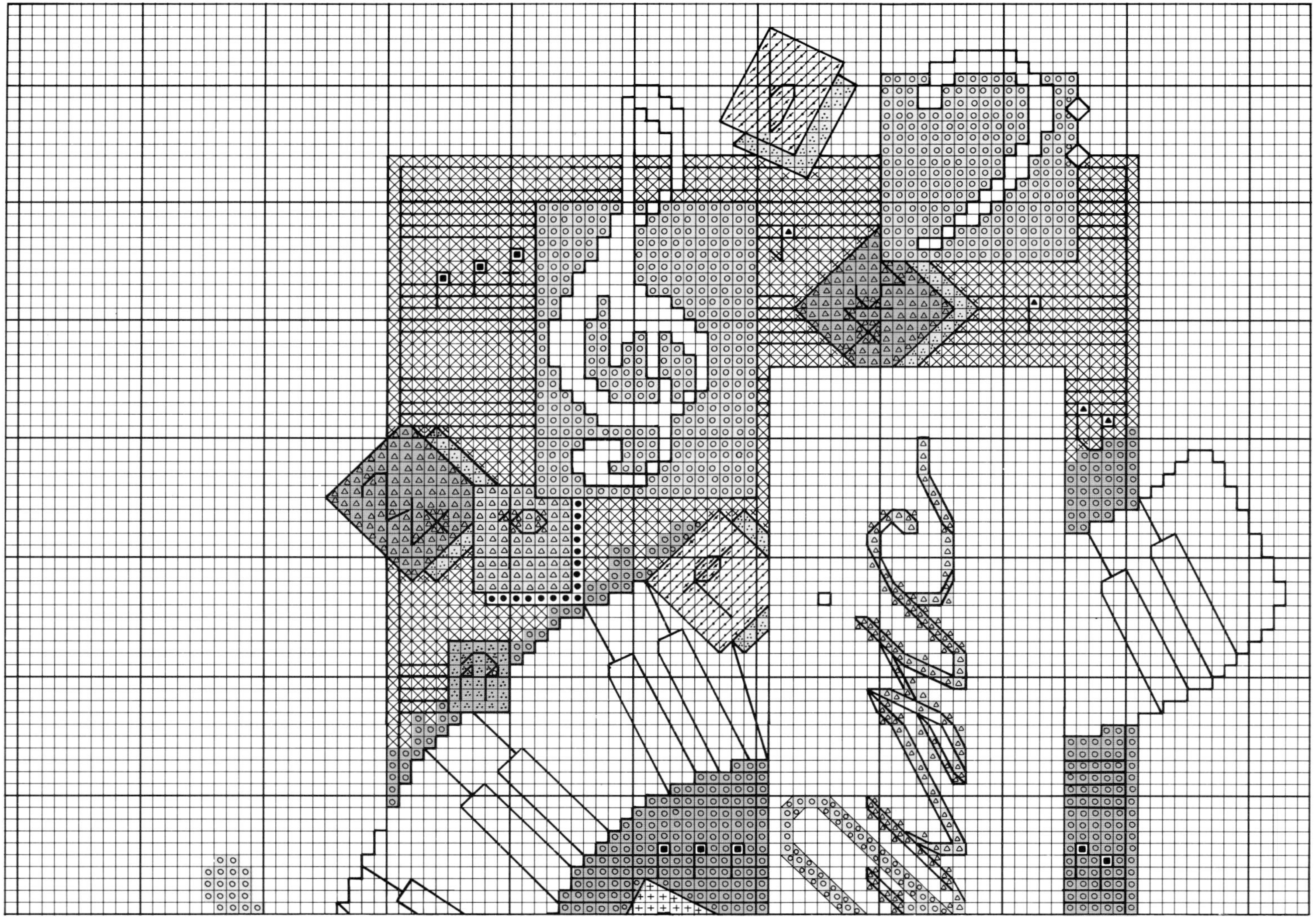

All That Jazz

SAMPLE
Stitched on ivory Belfast Linen 32 over 2 threads, the finished design size is 6⅜" x 9⅞". The fabric was cut 13" x 16".

FABRICS	DESIGN SIZES
Aida 11	9¼" x 14⅜"
Aida 14	7¼" x 11¼"
Aida 18	5⅝" x 8¾"
Hardanger 22	4⅝" x 7⅛"

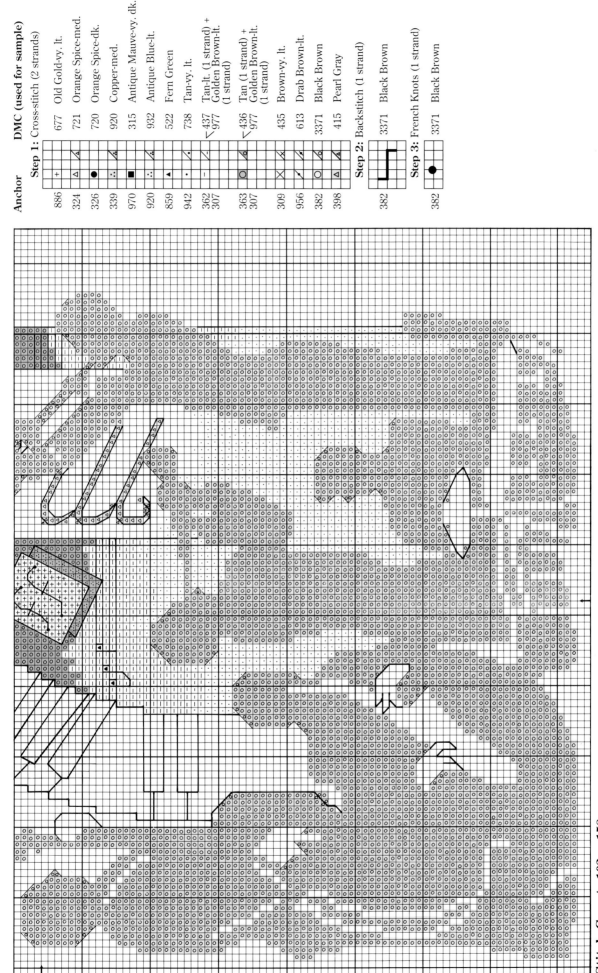

Stitch Count: 102 x 158

SEPTEMBER 15
National Weather Vane Day

This day marks the anniversary of the creation of the world's largest weather vane. Situated in Montague, Michigan, it is 48 feet high, has a 26-foot wind arrow, and weighs 3,500 pounds. Our weather vane is certainly much smaller, but it and the clock are sure to enhance your country collectibles.

Collectors' Box

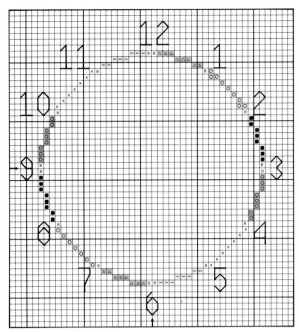

Stitch Count: 46 x 50

SAMPLE

Stitched on sand Dublin Linen 25 over 2 threads, the finished design size is 3⅝″ x 4″ for clock and 5⅜″ x 5⅜″ for weather vane. The fabric was cut 7″ x 7″ for clock and 9″ x 9″ for weather vane. After stitching is completed for clock, trim design piece to a 4⅝″-diameter circle. See Suppliers for collectors' box.

Clock

FABRICS	DESIGN SIZES
Aida 11	4⅛″ x 4½″
Aida 14	3¼″ x 3⅝″
Aida 18	2½″ x 2¾″
Hardanger 22	2⅛″ x 2¼″

Weather Vane

FABRICS	DESIGN SIZES
Aida 11	6⅛″ x 6⅛″
Aida 14	4¾″ x 4¾″
Aida 18	3¾″ x 3¾″
Hardanger 22	3″ x 3″

Stitch Count: 67 x 67

Anchor			DMC	(used for sample)
Step 1: Cross-stitch (2 strands)				
301	·	╱	744	Yellow-pale
306	O		725	Topaz
307	■		977	Golden Brown-lt.
4146	△		754	Peach-lt.
868	G		758	Terra Cotta-lt.
323	✕		722	Orange Spice-lt.
324	◎		721	Orange Spice-med.
5975	K		356	Terra Cotta-med.
870	∴		3042	Antique Violet-lt.
849	–		927	Slate Green-med.
921	+		931	Antique Blue-med.
922	●		930	Antique Blue-dk.
842	⦂		3013	Khaki Green-lt.
8581	S		647	Beaver Gray-med.
378	–		841	Beige Brown-lt.
380	B		839	Beige Brown-dk.

Step 2: Backstitch (1 strand)

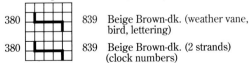

380	839	Beige Brown-dk. (weather vane, bird, lettering)
380	839	Beige Brown-dk. (2 strands) (clock numbers)

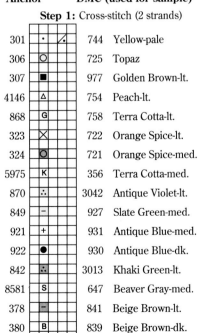

99

SEPTEMBER 23
Harvest Moon Ball

Remember that romantic evening—dancing by the light of the harvest moon? This whimsical design displayed on a keepsake box will bring back memories of magical fall nights.

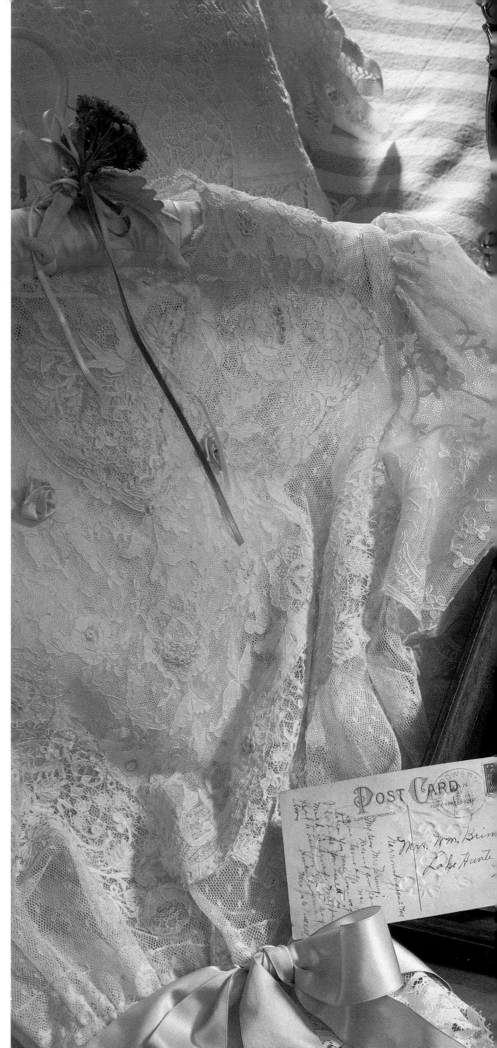

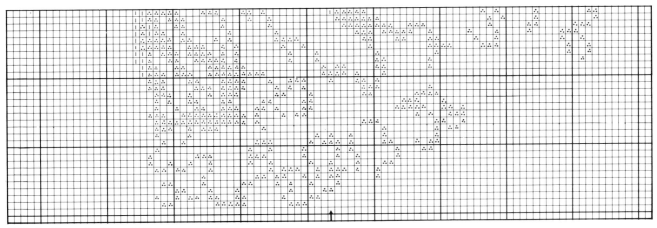

Stitch Count: 93 x 142

Moonlight Dancing

SAMPLE
Stitched on dirty linen Linda 27 over 2 threads, the finished design size is 6⅞" x 10½". The fabric was cut 13" x 17".

FABRIC	DESIGN SIZES
Aida 11	8½" x 12⅞"
Aida 14	6⅝" x 10⅛"
Aida 18	5⅛" x 7⅞"
Hardanger 22	4¼" x 6½"

DIRECTIONS
1. Have a professional framer assist in the construction of your box.

2. To make lid of box, have framer frame your design with a narrow molding (just as if it were going to be hung on the wall).

3. To make bottom of box, have framer construct a box to fit your framed piece, using 4 lengths of molding wider than the frame molding. Molding should be turned so that front faces outward and narrow lip forms resting place for lid. To finish box, have framer staple a piece of mat board to bottom. Place lid of box in recessed edge of box bottom.

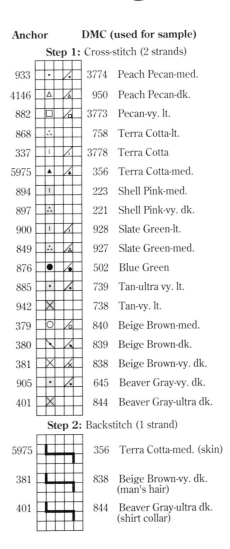

Anchor				DMC (used for sample)	
Step 1: Cross-stitch (2 strands)					
933	·		⟋	3774	Peach Pecan-med.
4146	△		⟋	950	Peach Pecan-dk.
882	▢		⟋	3773	Pecan-vy. lt.
868	∴			758	Terra Cotta-lt.
337	I		⟋	3778	Terra Cotta
5975	▲		⟋	356	Terra Cotta-med.
894	I			223	Shell Pink-med.
897	∵			221	Shell Pink-vy. dk.
900	I		⟋	928	Slate Green-lt.
849	∵		⟋	927	Slate Green-med.
876	●		⟋	502	Blue Green
885	·		⟋	739	Tan-ultra vy. lt.
942	⊠			738	Tan-vy. lt.
379	○		⟋	840	Beige Brown-med.
380	⟍		⟋	839	Beige Brown-dk.
381	⊠		⟋	838	Beige Brown-vy. dk.
905	·		⟋	645	Beaver Gray-vy. dk.
401	⊠			844	Beaver Gray-ultra dk.
Step 2: Backstitch (1 strand)					
5975				356	Terra Cotta-med. (skin)
381				838	Beige Brown-vy. dk. (man's hair)
401				844	Beaver Gray-ultra dk. (shirt collar)

OCTOBER 1–2
Apple Harvest Festival

Whether Granny Smith, golden delicious, or Jonathan, apples are America's favorite fruit. Celebrate with an apple a day and this cheerful basket bib.

Basket Bib

SAMPLE

Stitched on white Aida 14, the finished design size is 3⅜″ x 4¾″. The fabric was cut 7″ x 9″.

FABRICS	DESIGN SIZES
Aida 11	4¼″ x 6⅛″
Aida 18	2⅝″ x 3¾″
Hardanger 22	2⅛″ x 3″

MATERIALS

Completed cross-stitch on white Aida 14; matching thread
1 (5½″ x 7″) piece of white fabric for backing
1 (5½″ x 7″) piece of polyester fleece
¼ yard of blue/white print fabric
¾ yard of small cording
¾ yard (½″-wide) white eyelet
3 yards (1″-wide) white ribbon

DIRECTIONS

All seam allowances are ¼″.

1. With design centered, trim design piece to 5½″ x 7″.

2. From blue/white print fabric, cut 1″-wide bias strips, piecing as needed to equal 24″. To make corded piping, refer to page 65, step 2.

3. Pin fleece to wrong side of design piece. Baste piping to eyelet. With raw edges aligned, baste piping/eyelet to right side of design piece, rounding corners slightly. Trim corners and fleece.

4. With right sides facing, pin front to back. Stitch along edges, leaving an opening for turning. Clip corners and turn. Slipstitch opening closed. Turn under ¼″ on 1 end of each ribbon. Slipstitch to back of bib.

5. Use remaining piece of ribbon to wrap around back of basket and tie to bib ribbons to hold bib on basket (see photograph).

Stitch Count: 47 x 67

Anchor			DMC (used for sample)	
Step 1: Cross-stitch (2 strands)				
1	O	◢		White
891	X	◣	676	Old Gold-lt.
4146	–	◿	754	Peach-lt.
10	△	◹	352	Coral-lt.
11	∴	◿	350	Coral-med.
19	●	◢	817	Coral Red-vy. dk.
160	∴	◿	813	Blue-lt.
131	X		798	Delft-dk.
246	▲	◿	319	Pistachio Green-vy. dk.

Step 2: Satin Stitch (1 strand) (Refer to photo for color placement.)

42	▥	3350	Dusty Rose-vy. dk.
131	▥	798	Delft-dk.
349	▤	301	Mahogany-med.
371	▥	433	Brown-med.

Step 3: Long Stitch (1 strand)

215		320	Pistachio Green-med.

Step 4: Backstitch (1 strand)

11		350	Coral-med. (mouth, nose, chin)
131		798	Delft-dk. (ribbon, dress, pants)
371		433	Brown-med. (all else)

Step 5: French Knot (1 strand)

131	●	798	Delft-dk.

OCTOBER 9
Leif Erikson Day

October 9 is a good day to explore history and discover the important people from our past. On this date in the year 1000, North America was discovered by a Norse explorer. This colorful Viking ship design is a striking way to remember our heritage and honor the achievements of Leif Erikson.

Stitch Count: 74 x 74

Viking Ship

SAMPLE
Stitched on ivory Aida 14, finished design size is 5¼" x 5¼". The fabric was cut 12" x 12".

FABRICS

DESIGN SIZES

Aida 11   6¾" x 6¾"
Aida 18   4⅛" x 4⅛"
Hardanger 22   3⅜" x 3⅜"

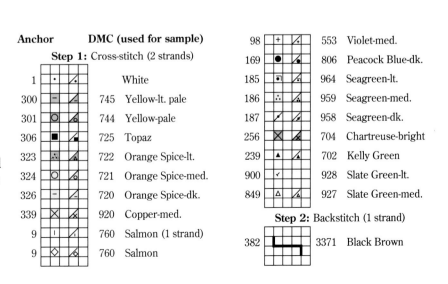

Anchor			DMC (used for sample)
			Step 1: Cross-stitch (2 strands)
1			White
300			745 Yellow-lt. pale
301			744 Yellow-pale
306			725 Topaz
323			722 Orange Spice-lt.
324			721 Orange Spice-med.
326			720 Orange Spice-dk.
339			920 Copper-med.
9			760 Salmon (1 strand)
9			760 Salmon

Anchor			DMC
98			553 Violet-med.
169			806 Peacock Blue-dk.
185			964 Seagreen-lt.
186			959 Seagreen-med.
187			958 Seagreen-dk.
256			704 Chartreuse-bright
239			702 Kelly Green
900			928 Slate Green-lt.
849			927 Slate Green-med.

Step 2: Backstitch (1 strand)

382		3371 Black Brown

107

Halloween

Stir up a ghastly spook this Halloween with a wicked witch windsock. For all the little ghosts and goblins trick-or-treating, it's sure to add a chill to the air.

Wicked Windsock

SAMPLE
Stitched on Waste Canvas 10, the finished design size is 5⅛" x 7⅝". The canvas was cut 7" x 10". The fabric was cut 15" x 22".

FABRICS	DESIGN SIZES
Aida 11	4⅝" x 6⅞"
Aida 14	3⅝" x 5½"
Aida 18	2⅞" x 4¼"
Hardanger 22	2⅜" x 3½"

MATERIALS
Completed cross-stitch on green waterproof rip-stop fabric; matching thread
1½ yards of black waterproof rip-stop fabric; matching thread
⅝ yard (1"-wide) belting
9¾ yards (1/16"-wide) rayon braid
White dressmakers' pencil
Large-eyed needle

DIRECTIONS
All seam allowances are ½".

1. With design centered, trim green fabric to 14" x 21½". From black fabric, cut 1 (17¼" x 21½") piece for hat; cut 1 (6" x 43") strip for hat ruffle; cut 1 (11" x 43") strip for collar ruffle; and cut 11 (2¾" x 30") strips for streamers.

2. With right sides facing, stitch the 14" edges of design piece together to make tube. Trim seam to ¼". Repeat with hat piece, stitching the 17¼" edges together. Finish top edge of hat by folding ¼" to wrong side and stitching.

3. Overlap ends of belting 1" and stitch overlapped ends together. Place belting on wrong side at top of hat. Fold top hemmed edge of hat over belting. Stitch hemmed edge to hat, making a 1½" casing.

4. To make hat ruffle, with wrong sides facing, fold 6" x 43" strip in half lengthwise. Stitch ends together. Stitch 2 rows of gathering stitches, ¼" apart, around long raw edge of ruffle. Gather ruffle to fit bottom of hat. With raw edges aligned and ruffle seam aligned with hat seam in back, stitch ruffle to right side of hat bottom.

5. With right sides facing, raw edges and seams aligned, and ruffle sandwiched between, stitch top of green tube to bottom of hat, sewing on ruffle stitching line. Stitch again, ¼" from edge.

6. To make collar ruffle, follow instructions in Step 4 to gather 11" x 43" strip to fit bottom of green tube. With raw edges and seams aligned, stitch collar ruffle to right side at bottom of green tube.

7. To make streamers, cut 1 end of each 2¾" x 30" strip to a point. Finish long edges and points by turning under ¼" and stitching a narrow hem. With raw edges aligned, pin straight edge of streamers over collar ruffle, overlapping ¼" on each side and adjusting as needed to fit around bottom edge of green tube. Stitch streamers to tube, sewing on ruffle stitching line. Stitch again, ¼" from edge.

8. For hanger, with white pencil, mark 4 points (2 on front, 2 on back), about 3½" in from each side at top of hat, just above stitching line for casing. Cut 8 (44") lengths of braid.

Thread needle with 2 lengths

of braid forming a loop at 1 end (Diagram 1). Bring needle through 1 marked point (Diagram 2), leaving a 1″ loop on other side. Remove needle. Run all 4 loose ends through loop and pull ends to tighten loop. Repeat at remaining 3 marks. Knot all free ends of braid together at top of windsock.

Diagram 1

1″ loop

Diagram 2

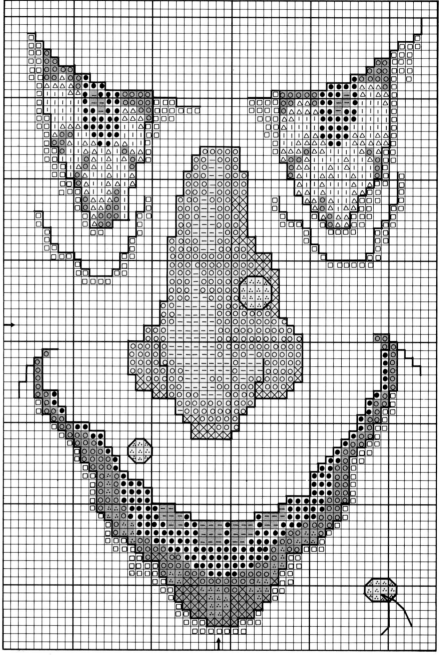

Stitch Count: 51 x 76

Anchor		DMC (used for sample)	
Step 1: Cross-stitch (6 strands)			
306	I	725	Topaz
307	△	977	Golden Brown-lt.
308	◉	976	Golden Brown-med.
355	⊠	975	Golden Brown-dk.
349	⦂	921	Copper
874	−	834	Olive Green-vy. lt.
889	◯ ◿	831	Olive Green-med.
906	⊠ ◿	829	Olive Green-vy. dk.
862	□	520	Fern Green-dk.
370	⦂ ◿	434	Brown-lt.
903	▦	3032	Mocha Brown-med.
403	●	310	Black
Step 2: Backstitch (2 strands)			
403	└─	310	Black

110

NOVEMBER 15
Silver Bells in the City

On this night, Michigan's capital city, Lansing, lights up with the warmth of hospitality as well as 3,000 candles lining the streets! Lansing initiated this holiday, to be celebrated with lights, music, and good cheer.

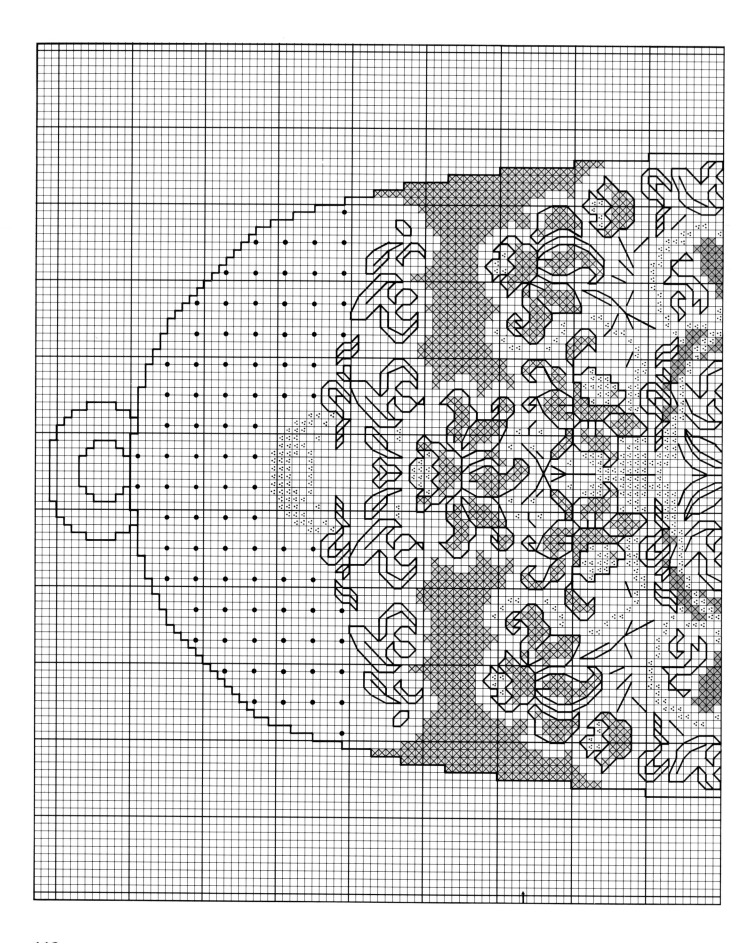

Stitch Count: 108 x 129

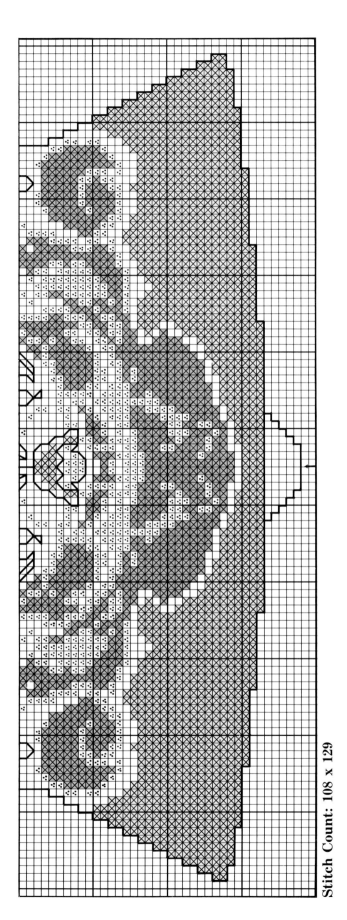

Silver Bells

SAMPLE

Stitched on pewter Murano 30 over 2 threads, the finished design size is 7¼" x 8⅝". The fabric was cut 14" x 15". See Suppliers for Mill Hill Beads.

FABRICS	DESIGN SIZES
Aida 11	9⅞" x 11¾"
Aida 14	7¾" x 9¼"
Aida 18	6" x 7⅛"
Hardanger 22	4⅞" x 5⅞"

DMC   **Marlitt (used for sample)**

Step 1: Cross-stitch (1 strand of each)

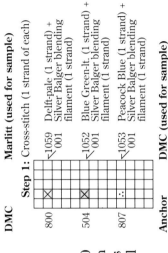

800	⌐1059	Delft-pale (1 strand) +
	001	Silver Balger blending filament (1 strand)
504	⌐1052	Blue Green-lt. (1 strand) +
	001	Silver Balger blending filament (1 strand)
807	⌐1053	Peacock Blue (1 strand) +
	001	Silver Balger blending filament (1 strand)

Anchor   **DMC (used for sample)**

Step 2: Backstitch (1 strand of each)

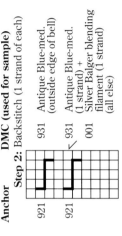

921	931	Antique Blue-med. (outside edge of bell)
921	⌐931	Antique Blue-med. (1 strand) +
	001	Silver Balger blending filament (1 strand) (all else)

Step 3: Beadwork

● 02010   Ice

Thanksgiving

Thanksgiving is a time when family and friends gather together to share in a celebration of thanks. It is a time to reflect on past blessings and show our appreciation for those dear to us. These beautiful stitched pieces will be a reminder of the spirit of this holiday all year long.

Runner

SAMPLE

Stitched on Vanessa-Ann Afghan Weave 18. The fabric was cut 24″ x 58″ (the width measurement includes 3 whole blocks and ½ block on each side). The stitching area of each woven block is 88 x 88. The heavy black lines surrounding each graph indicate the block boundaries. (See Diagram for placement.) See Suppliers for Overture yarns.

MATERIALS

Completed cross-stitch on Vanessa-Ann Afghan Weave 18; matching thread
5 skeins Overture yarn, Spices (color #V58)
Size #4 steel crochet hook

DIRECTIONS

1. To hem runner, turn under ½″ twice along all raw edges, mitering corners. Slipstitch hem in place.

2. *Note:* See page 121 for crochet abbreviations. Separate yarn into 4 single strands. Work first row of crochet stitches under 2 or 3 threads of fabric at folded edge of hem. *Row 1:* With runner turned to work across cross-stitched end, join 1 strand of yarn in corner, sc in same place, * ch 5, sk 13 or 14 threads, sc between next 2 threads, rep from * across, end with sc in corner = 30 sc and 29 ch-5 sps. Turn. *Row 2:* Sl st into ch-5 sp, ch 3 for first dc, 3 dc in same sp, * ch 3, 4 dc in next sp, rep from * across = 29 4-dc groups. Turn. *Row 3: Beginning half-triangle:* Ch 6 for first dc and ch 3, 4 dc in next sp, ch 3, 4 dc in next sp, turn, sl st into next ch-3 sp, ch 3 for dc, 3 dc in same sp, ch 3, 4 dc in next sp, turn, ch 6 for dc and ch 3, 4 dc in next sp. Fasten off. *Triangle:* Sk next 4-dc group on row 2, join yarn in next ch-3 sp, ch 3 for first dc, 3 dc in same sp, (ch 3, 4 dc in next sp) 7 times, turn, * sl st into next ch-3 sp, ch 3 for first dc, 3 dc in same sp, (ch 3, 4 dc in next sp) across, turn, rep from * 5 times more. Fasten off. Rep triangle as established twice more. *Ending half-triangle:* Sk next 4-dc group on row 2, join yarn in next ch-3 sp, ch 3 for first dc, 3 dc in same sp, ch 3, 4 dc in next sp, ch 3, sk 3 dc, dc in next dc, turn, ch 3 for dc, 3 dc in sp, ch 3, 4 dc in next sp, turn, sl st into next ch-3 sp, ch 3 for dc, 3 dc in same sp, ch 3, sk 3 dc, dc in next dc. Fasten off.

3. For each tassel, cut 5 (18″) strands of yarn (do not separate plies). Make 5 tassels. Knot a tassel in the ch-3 sp at the point of each triangle and half triangle.

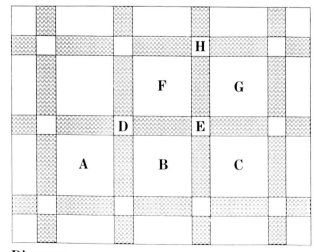

Diagram

Anchor		DMC (used for sample)	
		Step 1: Cross-stitch (2 strands)	
300	Z	745	Yellow-lt. pale
293	✓	727	Topaz-vy. lt.
293 265	✗	727 3348	Topaz-vy. lt. (1 strand) + Yellow Green-lt. (1 strand)
293 8	=	727 353	Topaz-vy. lt. (1 strand) + Peach (1 strand)
295	G	726	Topaz-lt.
306	R	725	Topaz
891	W	676	Old Gold-lt.
881	+	945	Peach Beige
8	J	353	Peach
10	◇	352	Coral-lt.
11	N	350	Coral-med.
13	F	349	Coral-dk.
9	∴	3712	Salmon-med.
316	•	971	Pumpkin
324	I	721	Orange Spice-med.
326	O	720	Orange Spice-dk.
347	S	402	Mahogany-vy. lt.
323	U	922	Copper-lt.
339	X	920	Copper-med.
46	⊡	666	Christmas Red-bright
47	M	321	Christmas Red
42	△	335	Rose
59	X	326	Rose-vy. dk.
20	◆	498	Christmas Red-dk.
44	●	815	Garnet-med.
43	+	3350	Dusty Rose-dk.
69	•	3687	Mauve
70	X	3685	Mauve-dk.
970	☐	315	Antique Mauve-vy. dk.
101	△	327	Antique Violet-vy. dk.
89 101	U	915 327	Plum-dk. (1 strand) + Antique Violet-vy. dk. (1 strand)

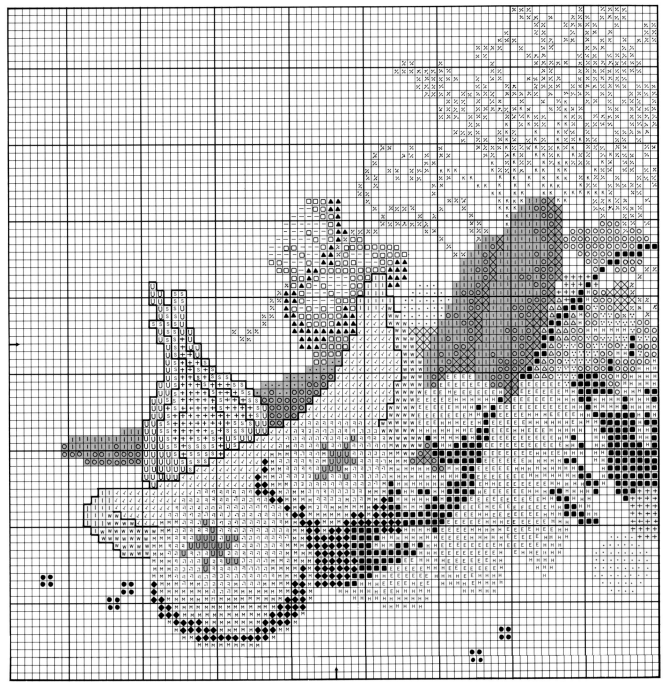

Stitch Count: 84 x 86 (section A)

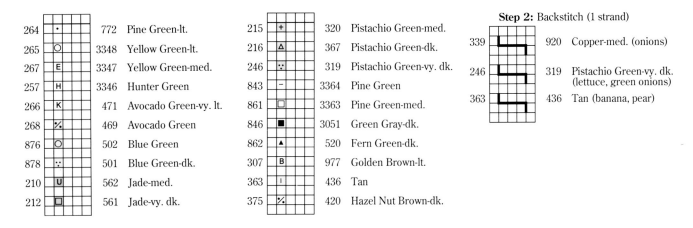

264	·	772	Pine Green-lt.
265	O	3348	Yellow Green-lt.
267	E	3347	Yellow Green-med.
257	H	3346	Hunter Green
266	K	471	Avocado Green-vy. lt.
268	⁒	469	Avocado Green
876	O	502	Blue Green
878	⁖	501	Blue Green-dk.
210	U	562	Jade-med.
212	▢	561	Jade-vy. dk.

215	+	320	Pistachio Green-med.
216	△	367	Pistachio Green-dk.
246	⁖	319	Pistachio Green-vy. dk.
843	–	3364	Pine Green
861	▢	3363	Pine Green-med.
846	■	3051	Green Gray-dk.
862	▲	520	Fern Green-dk.
307	B	977	Golden Brown-lt.
363	I	436	Tan
375	⁒	420	Hazel Nut Brown-dk.

Step 2: Backstitch (1 strand)

339	920	Copper-med. (onions)
246	319	Pistachio Green-vy. dk. (lettuce, green onions)
363	436	Tan (banana, pear)

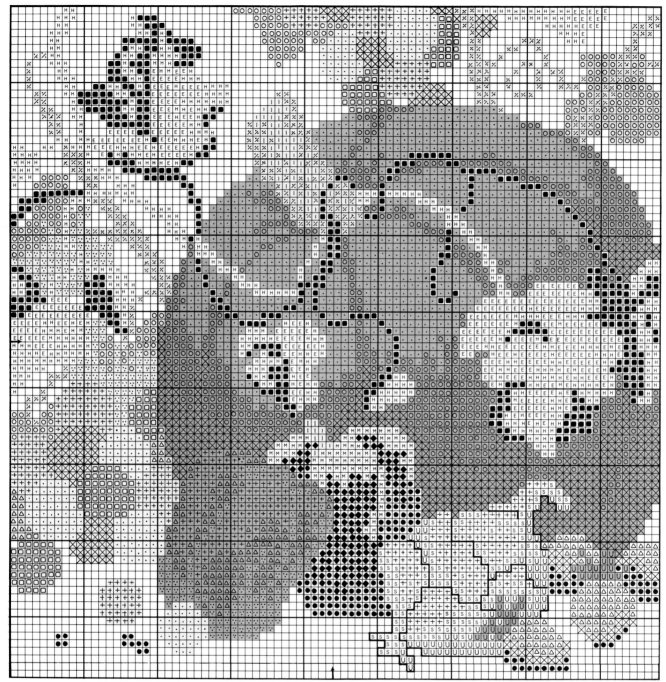

Stitch Count: 88 x 87 (section B)

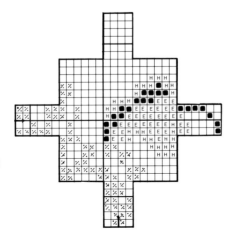

**Stitch Count: 28 x 20
(section D)**

118

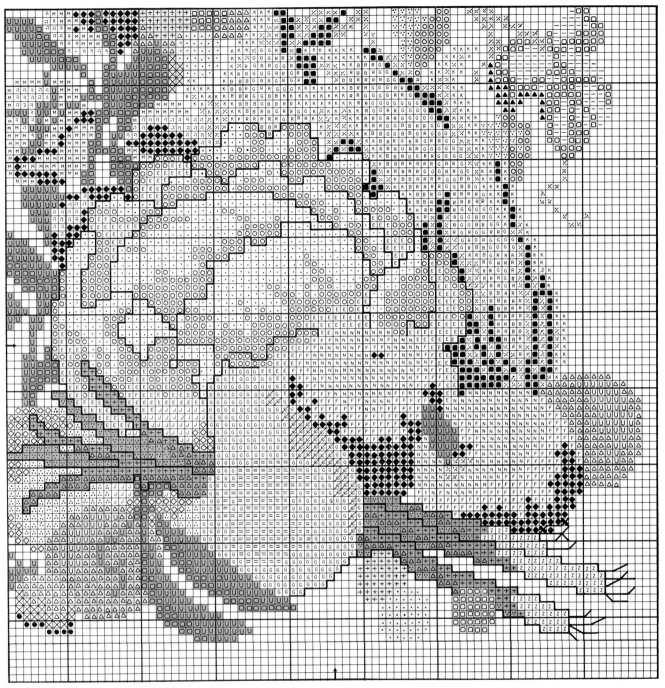

Stitch Count: 86 x 83 (section C)

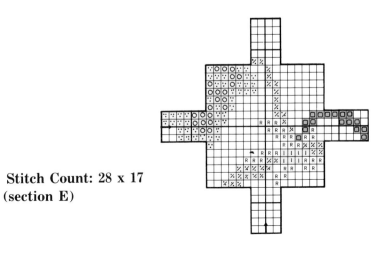

Stitch Count: 28 x 17
(section E)

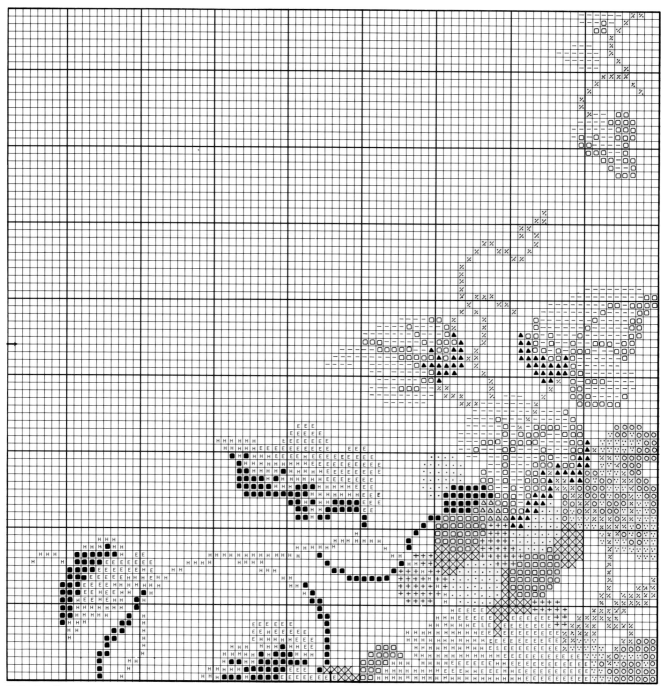

Stitch Count: 85 x 88 (section F)

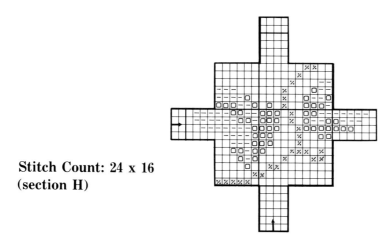

**Stitch Count: 24 x 16
(section H)**

120

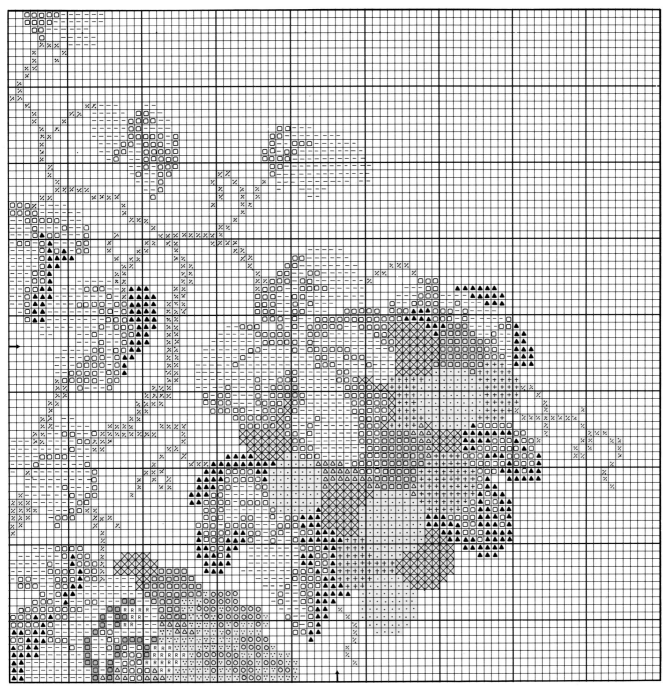

Stitch Count: 83 x 88 (section G)

CROCHET ABBREVIATIONS

ch—chain
dc—double crochet
rep—repeat
sc—single crochet
sk—skip
sl st—slip stitch
sp(s)—space(s)

God's Grace

SAMPLE
Stitched on ivory Aida 14, the finished design size is 7″ x 10″. The fabric was cut 13″ x 16″.

FABRICS	DESIGN SIZES
Aida 11	8⅛″ x 12¾″
Aida 18	5⅛″ x 7¾″
Hardanger 22	4½″ x 6⅜″

Anchor			DMC	(used for sample)

Step 1: Cross-stitch (2 strands)

Anchor			DMC	Color
1	+			White
316	｜		740	Tangerine
332	△		946	Burnt Orange-med.
307	–		977	Golden Brown-lt.
324	○	◢	922	Copper-lt.
339	∴		920	Copper-med.
349	■	◢	921	Copper
341	✕		919	Red Copper
42	–		335	Rose
59	○	◢	326	Rose-vy. dk.
47	∴		321	Christmas Red
43	✕	◢	815	Garnet-med.
95	∕	∕	554	Violet-lt.
99	∴	◢	552	Violet-dk.
101	●	◢	550	Violet-vy. dk.
266	○		3347	Yellow Green-med.
257	✕	◢	3346	Hunter Green
215	∕		320	Pistachio Green-med.
246	▲	◢	319	Pistachio Green-vy. dk.

Step 2: Backstitch (1 strand)

Anchor		DMC	Color
339		920	Copper-med. (pumpkin)
246		319	Pistachio Green-vy. dk. (stems)

Step 3: French Knots (1 strand)

Anchor		DMC	Color
246	●	319	Pistachio Green-vy. dk.

Stitch Count: 98 x 140

DECEMBER 25
Christmas

Christmas brings out traditions everywhere. Some are practiced in similar ways around the world, while others are unique to *our* ways of celebrating the season. This year begin your own traditions by stitching these beautiful stockings. Surprise your true love with the "Twelve Days of Christmas" motifs or make a Hawaiian Father Christmas—*Kanaka Loka*.

Stockings

SAMPLES
Stitched on caramel Annabelle 28 over 2 threads, finished design size is 7⅞" x 13¼" for angels and 7⅞" x 12⅝" for soldiers. Fabric for each stocking was cut 12" x 17". See Suppliers for Mill Hill Beads.

Angels
FABRICS	DESIGN SIZES
Aida 11	10" x 16⅞"
Aida 14	7⅞" x 13¼"
Aida 18	6⅛" x 10¼"
Hardanger 22	5" x 8⅜"

Soldiers
FABRICS	DESIGN SIZES
Aida 11	10⅛" x 16⅛"
Aida 14	7⅞" x 12⅝"
Aida 18	6⅛" x 9⅞"
Hardanger 22	5" x 8"

MATERIALS (for 1 stocking)
Completed cross-stitch on caramel Annabelle 28; matching thread
1 (10" x 15") piece of unstitched caramel Annabelle 28 for stocking back and hanger loop
½ yard (45"-wide) tan fabric for lining and ruffle

DIRECTIONS
All seam allowances are ¼".

1. Enlarge pattern for stocking. For stocking front, place pattern on design piece with top edge of stocking 1" above and parallel to top row of stitching. Cut out.

2. From unstitched Annabelle, cut 1 stocking piece for back and 1 (4" x 2") piece for hanger.

3. From tan fabric, cut 2 stocking pieces for lining and 1¼"-wide bias strips for ruffle, piecing as needed to equal 96". Cut strip into 1 (70") piece and 1 (26") piece.

4. With wrong sides facing and raw edges aligned, fold 70" ruffle strip in half lengthwise to measure ⅝"-wide; press. Run a gathering thread ⅛" from raw edges. Gather ruffle to fit around sides and bottom edges of stocking front. With raw edges aligned, pin ruffle to right side of stocking front; baste. With right sides facing, stitch stocking front to back, leaving top edge open. Clip curves and turn.

5. Fold and gather 26" ruffle strip as above to fit around top of stocking. With raw edges aligned, pin ruffle around top edge on right side of stocking; baste.

6. To make hanger, with right sides facing and raw edges aligned, fold 4" x 2" Annabelle piece in half lengthwise to measure 4" x 1". Stitch along the 4" edge. Turn. Fold in half to form a loop. With raw edges aligned, pin ends to top left-hand edge of stocking on top of ruffle. Baste hanger in place.

7. With right sides facing, stitch lining front to back, leaving top open and an opening in side seam for turning. Clip curves. Do not turn. Slide lining over stocking, with right sides facing, side seams matching, and the ruffle and hanger at top of stocking sandwiched in between. Stitch around top edge of stocking, through all layers. Turn stocking right side out through opening in lining. Slip-stitch opening closed. Tuck lining inside stocking.

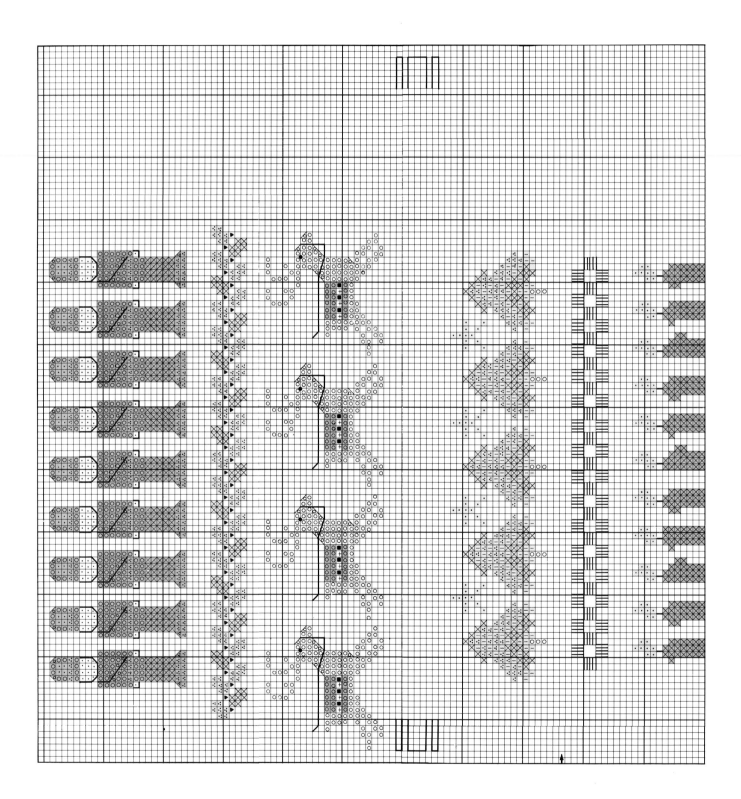

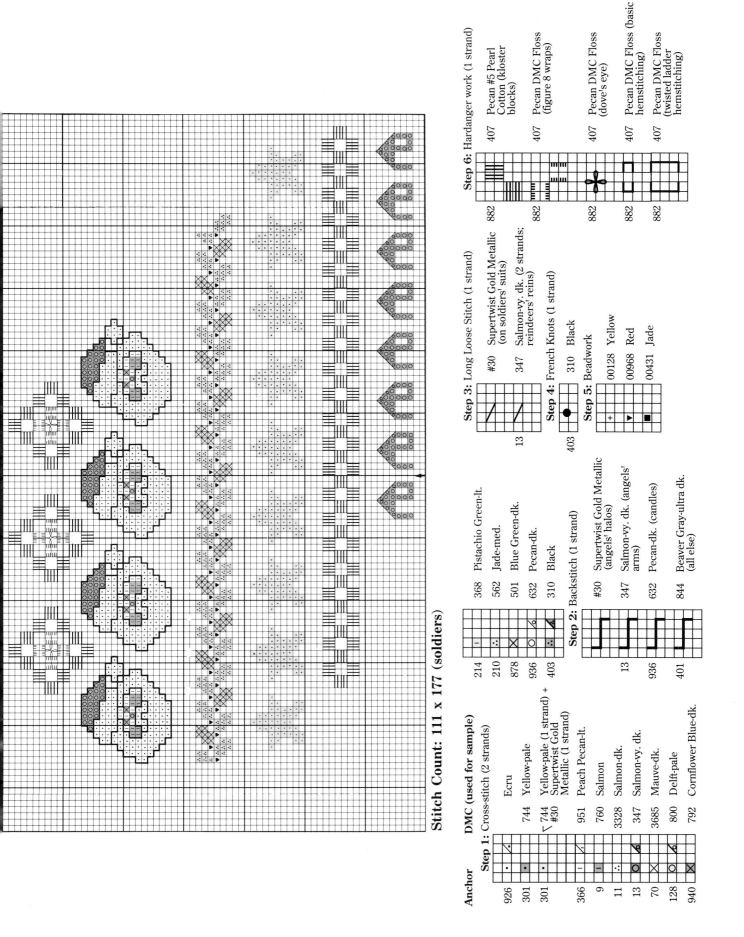

Stitch Count: 111 x 177 (soldiers)

Anchor   DMC (used for sample)

Step 1: Cross-stitch (2 strands)

Anchor		DMC	
926	·		Ecru
301	⊡	744	Yellow-pale
301	·	∨744	Yellow-pale (1 strand) + #30 Supertwist Gold Metallic (1 strand)
366	–	951	Peach Pecan-lt.
9	⁄	760	Salmon
11	∷	3328	Salmon-dk.
13	◔	347	Salmon-vy. dk.
70	✕	3685	Mauve-dk.
128	⊘	800	Delft-pale
940	⊠	792	Cornflower Blue-dk.
214	∣	368	Pistachio Green-lt.
210	∷	562	Jade-med.
878	⊠	501	Blue Green-dk.
936	◔	632	Pecan-dk.
403	▨	310	Black

Step 2: Backstitch (1 strand)

	#30	Supertwist Gold Metallic (angels' halos)
13	347	Salmon-vy. dk. (angels' arms)
936	632	Pecan-dk. (candles)
401	844	Beaver Gray-ultra dk. (all else)

Step 3: Long Loose Stitch (1 strand)

	#30	Supertwist Gold Metallic (on soldiers' suits)
13	347	Salmon-vy. dk. (2 strands; reindeers' reins)

Step 4: French Knots (1 strand)

403	310	Black

Step 5: Beadwork

+	00128	Yellow
▶	00968	Red
▣	00431	Jade

Step 6: Hardanger work (1 strand)

407	Pecan #5 Pearl Cotton (kloster blocks)
882	407 Pecan DMC Floss (figure 8 wraps)
882	407 Pecan DMC Floss (dove's eye)
882	407 Pecan DMC Floss (basic hemstitching)
882	407 Pecan DMC Floss (twisted ladder hemstitching)

127

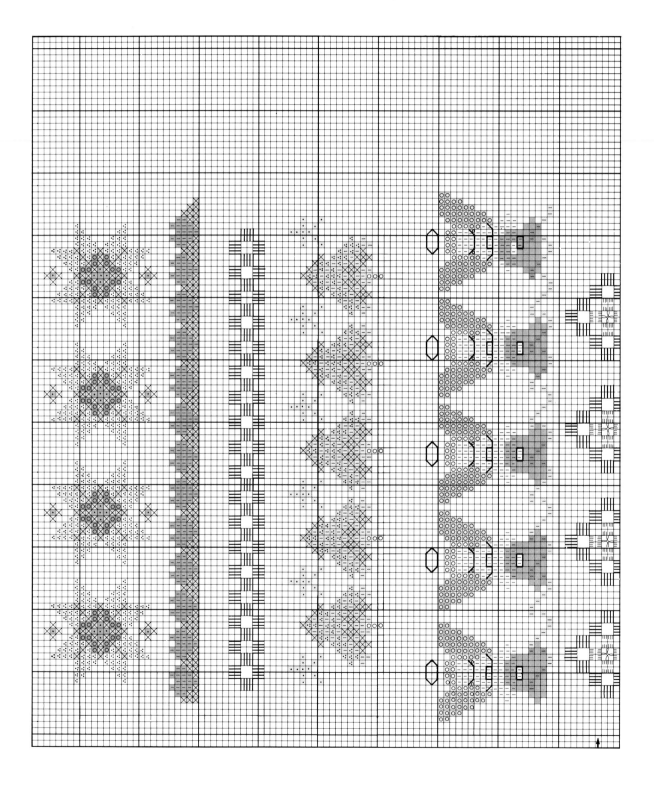

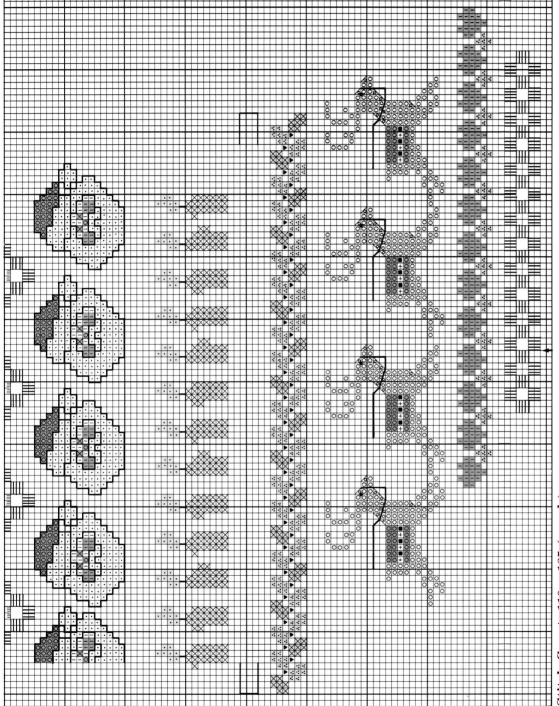

Stitch Count: 110 x 185 (angels)

Stocking Pattern
Each square = 1 inch.

Father Christmas

SAMPLE
Stitched on white Belfast Linen 32 over 2 threads, the finished design size is 8¼″ x 10¾″. The fabric was cut 15″ x 17″. See Suppliers for Balger cord metallics and blending filaments.

FABRICS	DESIGN SIZES
Aida 11	11⅞″ x 15¾″
Aida 14	9⅜″ x 12⅜″
Aida 18	7¼″ x 9⅝″
Hardanger 22	6″ x 7⅞″

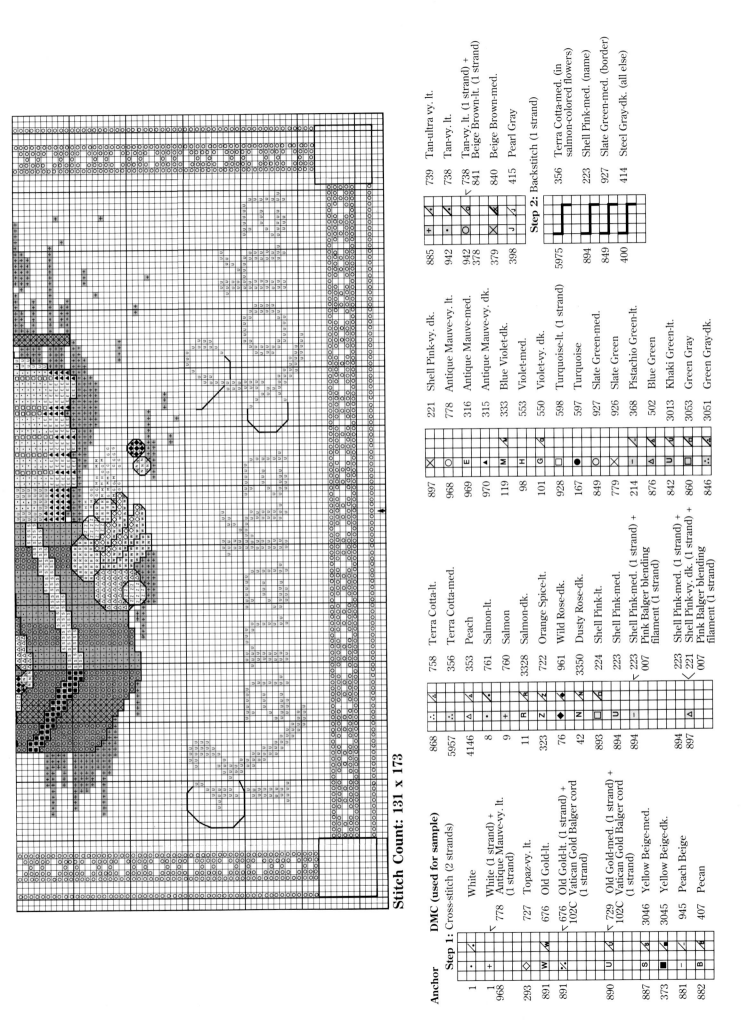

Stitch Count: 131 x 173

Step 1: Cross-stitch (2 strands)

Anchor	Symbol	DMC	Name
1	·		White
1	+		White (1 strand) +
968		778	Antique Mauve-vy. lt. (1 strand)
293	◇	727	Topaz-vy. lt.
891	W	676	Old Gold-lt.
891	⚡	676	Old Gold-lt. (1 strand) +
		102C	Vatican Gold Balger cord (1 strand)
890	U	729	Old Gold-med. (1 strand) +
		102C	Vatican Gold Balger cord (1 strand)
887	S	3046	Yellow Beige-med.
373	■	3045	Yellow Beige-dk.
881	−	945	Peach Beige
882	B	407	Pecan

Anchor	Symbol	DMC	Name
868	∴		Terra Cotta-lt.
5957	∴		Terra Cotta-med.
4146	△	353	Peach
8	·	761	Salmon-lt.
9	+	760	Salmon
11	R	3328	Salmon-dk.
323	Z	722	Orange Spice-lt.
76	◆	961	Wild Rose-dk.
42	N	3350	Dusty Rose-dk.
893	□	224	Shell Pink-lt.
894	U	223	Shell Pink-med.
894	−	223	Shell Pink-med. (1 strand) +
007			Pink Balger blending filament (1 strand)
894		223	Shell Pink-med. (1 strand) +
897	△	221	Shell Pink-vy. dk. (1 strand) +
007			Pink Balger blending filament (1 strand)

Anchor	Symbol	DMC	Name
897	⊠	221	Shell Pink-vy. dk.
968	○	778	Antique Mauve-vy. lt.
969	E	316	Antique Mauve-med.
970	◀	315	Antique Mauve-vy. dk.
119	M	333	Blue Violet-dk.
98	H	553	Violet-med.
101	G	550	Violet-vy. dk.
928	□	598	Turquoise-lt. (1 strand)
167	●	597	Turquoise
849	○	927	Slate Green-med.
779	⊠	926	Slate Green
214	∣	368	Pistachio Green-lt.
876	◁	502	Blue Green
842	U	3013	Khaki Green-lt.
860	□	3053	Green Gray
846	∴	3051	Green Gray-dk.

Anchor	Symbol	DMC	Name
885	+	739	Tan-ultra vy. lt.
942	·	738	Tan-vy. lt.
942	○	738	Tan-vy. lt. (1 strand) +
378		841	Beige Brown-lt. (1 strand)
379	⊠	840	Beige Brown-med.
398	J	415	Pearl Gray

Step 2: Backstitch (1 strand)

Anchor	DMC	Name
5975	356	Terra Cotta-med. (in salmon-colored flowers)
894	223	Shell Pink-med. (name)
849	927	Slate Green-med. (border)
400	414	Steel Gray-dk. (all else)

Anchor   DMC (used for sample)

Twelve Days of Christmas

FABRICS	DESIGN SIZES
Aida 11	3⅝" x 3⅝"
Aida 14	2⅞" x 2⅞"
Aida 18	2¼" x 2¼"
Hardanger 22	1⅞" x 1⅞"

SAMPLE

Stitched on white Hardanger 22 over 2 threads, the finished size for each design is 3⅝" x 3⅝". The fabric was cut 10" x 10" for each framed piece.

For the scroll, shown in photo, cut 1 (6" x 42") piece of fabric and stitch holly motif and 6 designs as follows. Begin stitching holly motif 1½" from 1 (6") end of fabric and 1¼" from 1 long edge. Repeat on opposite long edge (see photo). Then, from bottom of holly motif, skip the equivalent of 1 stitch, center Design 1, and begin stitching. After completing Design 1, skip the equivalent of 2 stitches and repeat procedure with the holly motif and next design, completing 5 more designs and finishing with holly motif. If desired, make 2d scroll as above, using Designs 7-12. See Suppliers for information on ordering scroll and easel.

MATERIALS (for 1 scroll)

Completed cross-stitch on white Hardanger 22
2½ yards (1"-wide) green satin ribbon; matching thread
1 purchased 6" wooden scroll frame
1 purchased 6" x 7⅝" wooden easel

DIRECTIONS

1. To bind long raw edges, cut 2 (42") pieces from ribbon. Fold ribbon in half lengthwise; press.

2. Insert 1 raw edge of design piece inside 1 length of folded ribbon. Machine-stitch along finished edge of ribbon, stitching through all 3 layers.

3. Following manufacturer's instructions, attach design piece to scroll.

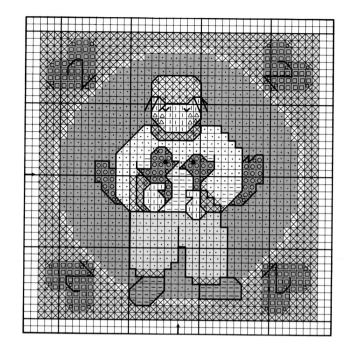

Stitch Count: 40 x 40 (for each design)

Anchor			DMC	(used for sample)

Step 1: Cross-stitch (3 strands)

Anchor			DMC	
1	·	⁄		White
295	−	⁄	726	Topaz-lt.
306	▨	⁄	725	Topaz
307	−	⁄	783	Christmas Gold
316	△	⁄	740	Tangerine
4146	ı	⁄	754	Peach-lt.
8	△	⁄	761	Salmon-lt.
27	◻	⁄	899	Rose-med.
42	○	⁄	309	Rose-deep
47	✕	⁄	321	Christmas Red
108	△	⁄	211	Lavender-lt.
110	◻	⁄	208	Lavender-vy. dk.
158	○	⁄	828	Blue-ultra vy. lt.
162	✕	⁄	825	Blue-dk.
204	▽	⁄	912	Emerald Green-lt.
923	·	⁄	699	Christmas Green
379	○	⁄	840	Beige Brown-med.
397	−	⁄	762	Pearl Gray-vy. lt.
400	✕		414	Steel Gray-dk.

Step 2: Backstitch (1 strand)

923		699	Christmas Green (veins in holly leaves)
236		3799	Pewter Gray-vy. dk. (everything except gold rings)

Step 3: Long Stitch (3 strands)

		002p	Gold Balger Cable (rings)

Step 4: French Knots (1 strand)

236	●	3799	Pewter Gray-vy. dk.

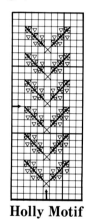

Holly Motif

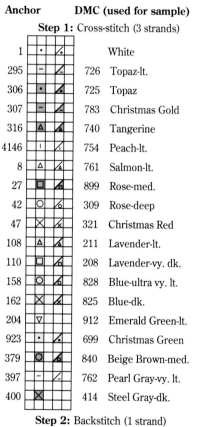

136

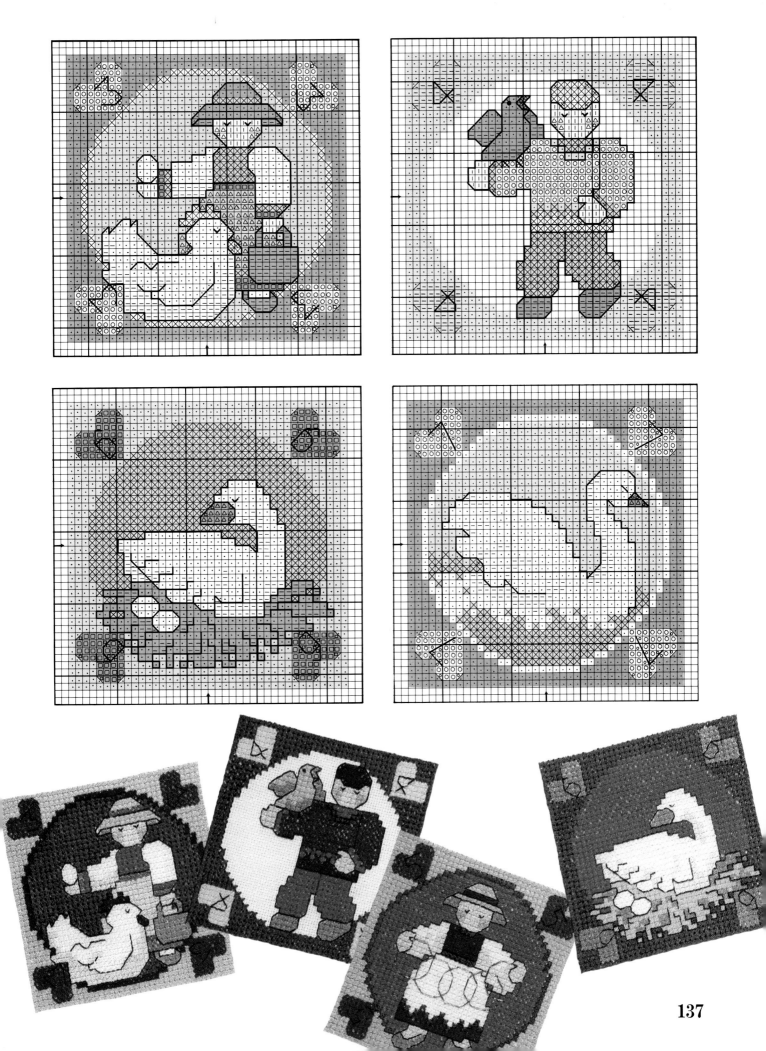

137

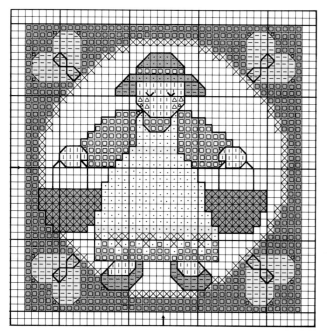

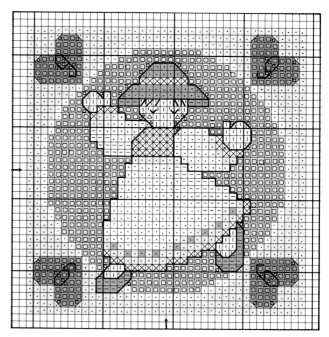

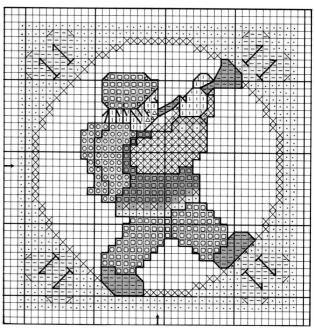

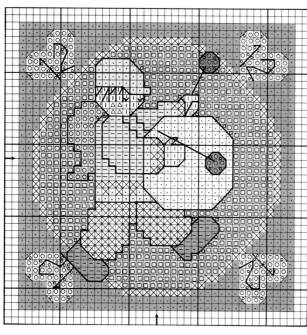

1. **Partridge in a Pear Tree**
2. **Turtledoves**
3. **French Hens**
4. **Calling Birds**
5. **Gold Rings**
6. **Geese a-Laying**
7. **Swans a-Swimming**
8. **Maids a-Milking**
9. **Ladies Dancing**
10. **Lords a-Leaping**
11. **Pipers Piping**
12. **Drummers Drumming**

General Instructions

Cross-Stitch

Fabrics: Most of the designs in this book are worked on even-weave fabrics made especially for cross-stitch and can be found in your local needlework shop. If you cannot find a particular fabric, see Suppliers for ordering information. Fabrics used in the models are identified in the sample information by color, name, and thread count per inch.

Preparing Fabric: Cut the fabric at least 3″ larger on all sides than the design size or cut it the size specified in the sample information. A 3″ margin is the minimum amount of fabric required to insure plenty of space for matting, framing, and other finishing techniques for your stitched piece. To keep fabric from fraying, whipstitch or machine-zigzag the raw edges or apply liquid ravel preventer and allow to dry.

Needles: Needles should slip easily through the holes but not pierce the fabric. With fabric that has 11 or fewer threads per inch, use needle size 24; with 14 threads per inch, use needle size 24 or 26; with 18 or more threads per inch, use needle size 26. Never leave the needle in the design area of your work. It can leave rust or a permanent impression on your fabric.

Finished Design Size: To determine what the finished size of the design will be, divide the stitch count by the threads per inch of the fabric. When designs are stitched over two threads, divide the stitch count by half the threads per inch.

Hoop or Frame: Select a hoop or stretcher bars large enough to hold the entire design. Working with a hoop or frame helps to keep the fabric taut and makes it easier to make uniform stitches. Place the screw or the clamp of the hoop in a 10 o'clock position (or 2 o'clock, if you are left-handed) to keep it from catching the floss.

Floss: Cut 18″ lengths of floss. For best coverage, separate the strands. Then put back together the number of strands called for in the color code.

Centering Design: To find the center of the fabric, fold it in half from top to bottom and then from left to right. The intersection of these folds is the center. To find the center of the design, follow the vertical and horizontal arrows until they intersect. Begin stitching at the center points of the graph and the fabric.

Securing Floss: Bring the needle and most of the floss up through the fabric, leaving a 1″ tail of floss on the underside of the fabric. Secure the loose floss with the first few stitches.

Another method for securing floss is the waste knot. Knot your floss and insert your needle from the right side of the fabric about 1″ from the design area. Work several stitches over the thread to secure. Cut off the knot.

To secure the floss when you are finished, run the needle under four or five stitches on the back of the design and clip the tail close to the fabric.

Stitching Method: For smooth stitches, use the push-and-pull method. Push the needle straight up through the fabric, pulling the floss completely through to the front of the fabric. Bring the needle to the back by pushing the needle straight down, pulling the needle and floss completely through to the back of the fabric. Do not pull the thread tight. For even stitches, the tension should be consistent throughout.

Carrying Floss: To carry floss, weave it under the previously worked stitches on the back. Do not carry your floss across any fabric that is not or will not be stitched. Loose strands, especially dark ones, will show through the fabric.

Twisted Floss: Floss covers best when lying flat. If the floss begins to twist, drop the needle and allow the floss to unwind itself. To keep floss from twisting and knotting during stitching, use strands no longer than 18″.

Cleaning Completed Work: When stitching is complete, soak the finished piece in cold water with a mild soap for 5 to 10 minutes. Rinse thoroughly. Roll work in a towel to remove excess water; do not wring. Place work face down on a dry towel and, with iron on warm setting, iron until work is dry.

Common Stitches

Cross-stitch: Make one cross for each symbol on the chart. Bring the needle and thread up at A, down at B, up at C, and down again at D (Diagram A). For rows, stitch from left to right, then back (Diagram B). All stitches in a row should lie in the same direction.

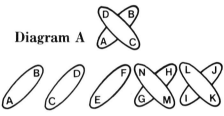

Diagram A

Diagram B

French Knot: Bring the needle up at A, using one strand of floss. Wrap the floss around the needle two times (unless indicated otherwise in instructions). Insert the needle beside A, pulling the floss until it fits snugly around the needle. Pull the needle through to the back (Diagram C).

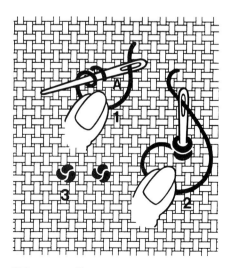

Diagram C

Backstitch: Complete all cross-stitching before working back-stitches or other accent stitches. Working from left to right with one strand of floss (unless indicated otherwise in the color code), bring the needle and the thread up at A, down at B, and up again at C. Going back down at A, continue in this manner (Diagram D).

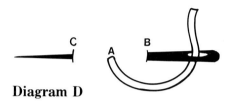

Diagram D

Half-cross: Half-cross is indicated on the graph with a slanted line and the color symbol beside it. Make the longer stitch in the direction of the slanted line on the graph. The stitch actually fills three-fourths of the area. Bring needle and thread up at A, down at B, up at C, and down at D (Diagram E).

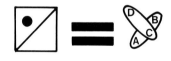

Diagram E

WASTE CANVAS

Cut the waste canvas 1″ larger on all sides than the finished design. Baste the waste canvas to the fabric to be stitched. Complete the stitching; each stitch is over one unit (two threads). When stitching is complete, use a spray bottle to dampen the stitched area with cold water. Pull the waste canvas threads out one at a time with tweezers. It is easier to pull all the threads running in one direction first; then pull out the opposite threads. Allow the stitching to dry; then place face down on a towel and iron.

Beadwork

First, attach the beads to the fabric with a diagonal stitch, lower left to upper right. Secure the beads by returning the floss through the beads, lower right to upper left (Diagram F). Complete the row of diagonal stitches before returning to secure all beads.

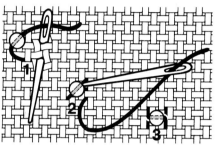

Diagram F

Sewing Hint

Bias Strips: Bias strips are used for ruffles, binding, or corded piping. To cut bias strips, fold the fabric at a 45-degree angle to the grain of the fabric and crease. Cut on the crease. Cut additional strips the width indicated in instructions and parallel to the first cutting line. The ends of the bias strips should be on the grain of the fabric. Place the right sides of the ends together and stitch with ¼″ seam. Continue to piece strips until they are the length indicated in instructions (Diagram G).

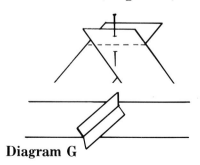

Diagram G

Special Stitches

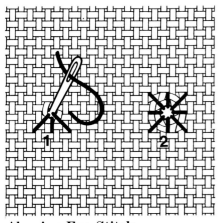

Algerian Eye Stitch

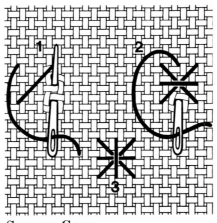

Smyrna Cross

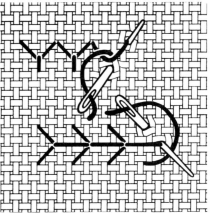

Fly Stitch (2 versions)

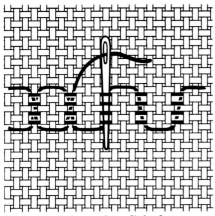

Threaded Running Stitch Variation

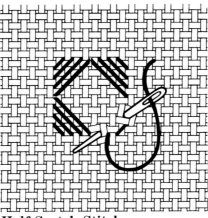

Half Scotch Stitch

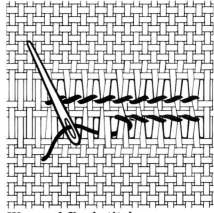

Wrapped Backstitch

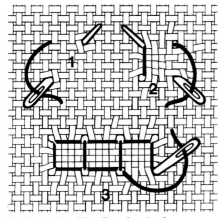

Pulled Trellis Backstitch

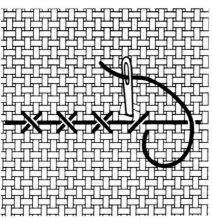

Couching with Cross-Stitch

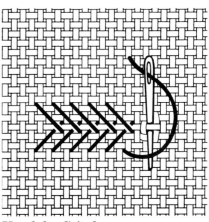

Vandyke Stitch

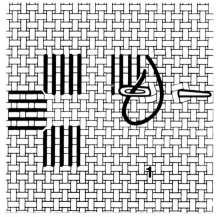

**Hardanger Work
Kloster Blocks**

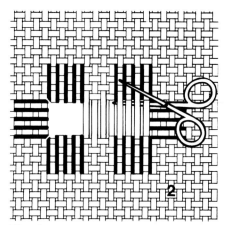

**Hardanger Work
Kloster Blocks**

**Hardanger Work
Figure Eights**

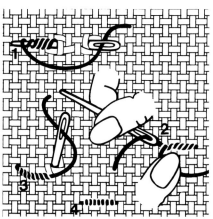

Bullion Stitch

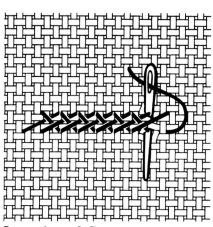

Long-Armed Cross

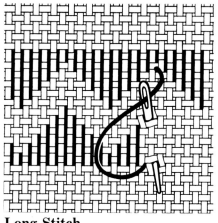

Long Stitch

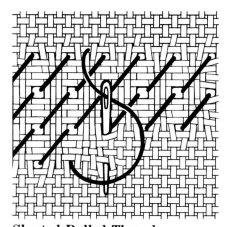

Slanted Pulled Thread

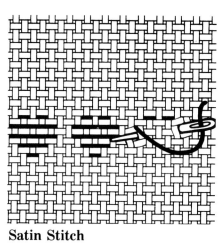

Satin Stitch

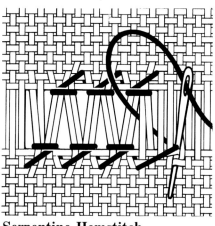

Serpentine Hemstitch

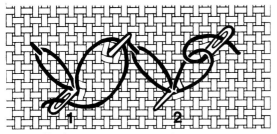

Lazy Daisy

Twisted Ladder Hemstitch

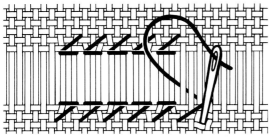

Basic Hemstitch

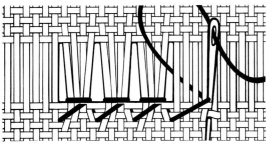

Ladder Hemstitch

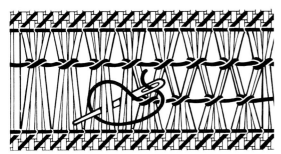

Double Twisted Hemstitch

Suppliers

All products are available retail from Shepherd's Bush, 220 24th Street, Ogden, UT 84401; (801) 399-4546; or for a merchant near you, write the following suppliers:

Zweigart Fabrics—Zweigart/Joan Toggitt Ltd., Weston Canal Plaza, 2 Riverview Drive, Somerset, NJ 08873

Zweigart Fabrics used:

White Aida 14	White Linda 27
Ivory Aida 14	Ivory Linda 27
Pink Aida 14	Celery Green Linda 27
White Gardasee 14	Dirty Linen Linda 27
White Undine 14	White Quaker Cloth 28
Rustico 14	Caramel Annabelle 28
White Aida 18	White Murano 30
Dawn Gray Damask Aida 18	Cracked Wheat Murano 30
White Hardanger 22	Pewter Murano 30
Raw Dublin Linen 25	White Belfast Linen 32
Sand Dublin Linen 25	Cream Belfast Linen 32
Wedgewood Lugana 25	Driftwood Belfast Linen 32

White Jobelan 28—Wichelt Imports, Inc., Rural Route 1, Stoddard, WI 54658

Waste Canvas 10—Charles Craft, P.O. Box 1049, Laurinburg, NC 28352

Glenshee Egyptian Cotton Quality D28—Anne Powell, P.O. Box 3060, Stuart, FL 34995

White Perforated Paper—Astor Place, 239 Main Avenue, Stirling, NJ 07980

Mill Hill Beads—Gay Bowles Sales, 1310 Plainfield Ave., Janesville, WI 53547

Balger Products, Gold Metallic Thread, Belding Buttonhole Silk Twist, Au Ver A Soie Silk Thread—Kreinik Mfg. Co., Inc., 1708 Gihon Road, Parkersburg, WV 26101

Glissen Gloss Sterling Threads—Madeira Marketing, 600 East 9th, Michigan City, IN 46360

Wild Threads—T.S. Designs, 249C Avenida del Norte, Redondo Beach, CA 90277

Broder Medicis Wool Yarn—The DMC Corp., Port Kearny Building #10, South Kearny, NJ 07032-0650

Ginnie Thompson Flower Thread—Craft World, P.O. Box 779, New Windsor, MD 21776

Collectors' Box (#CL6)—Sunshine Station, P.O. Drawer 2388, Hickory, NC 28603

Scroll and Easel—Tomorrow's Treasures, 19722 144th Avenue N.E., Woodenville, WA 98072

Overture Yarn—Rainbow Gallery, 13756 Victory Boulevard, Van Nuys, CA 91401

Jacket Motifs

Baby Chick

Anchor   **DMC (used for sample)**

Step 1: Cross-stitch (2 strands)

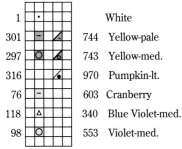

1		White
301		744 Yellow-pale
297		743 Yellow-med.
316		970 Pumpkin-lt.
76		603 Cranberry
118		340 Blue Violet-med.
98		553 Violet-med.

Step 2: Backstitch (1 strand)

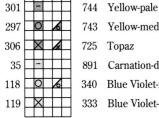

77		602 Cranberry-med. (easter egg)
914		3772 Pecan-med. (chick)

Step 3: French Knots (1 strand)

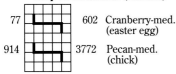

118	●	340 Blue Violet-med.

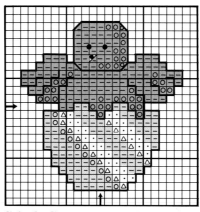

Stitch Count: 21 x 21

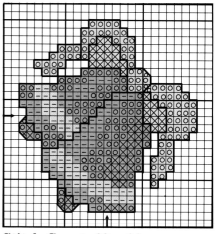

Stitch Count: 23 x 24

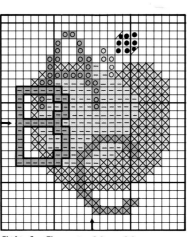

Stitch Count: 20 x 23

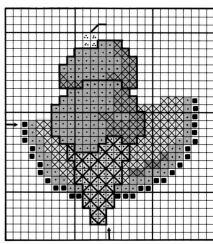

Stitch Count: 23 x 25

Bells

Anchor   **DMC (used for sample)**

Step 1: Cross-stitch (2 strands)

301		744 Yellow-pale
297		743 Yellow-med.
306		725 Topaz
35		891 Carnation-dk.
118		340 Blue Violet-med.
119		333 Blue Violet-dk.

Step 2: Backstitch (1 strand)

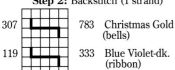

307		783 Christmas Gold (bells)
119		333 Blue Violet-dk. (ribbon)

ABC Apple

Anchor   **DMC (used for sample)**

Step 1: Cross-stitch (2 strands)

297		743 Yellow-med.
35		891 Carnation-dk.
13		349 Coral-dk.
118		340 Blue Violet-med.
239		702 Kelly Green
228		910 Emerald Green-dk.
914		3772 Pecan-med.

Step 2: Backstitch (1 strand)

307		783 Christmas Gold

Ice Cream Cone

Anchor   **DMC (used for sample)**

Step 1: Cross-stitch (2 strands)

386		746 Off White
300		745 Yellow-lt. pale
40		956 Geranium
35		891 Carnation-dk.
228		910 Emerald Green-dk.
307		977 Golden Brown-lt.

Step 2: Backstitch (1 strand)

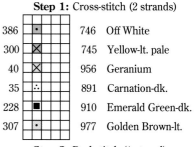

307		783 Christmas Gold (ice cream)
228		910 Emerald Green-dk. (cherry stem)
914		3772 Pecan-med. (inside cone)

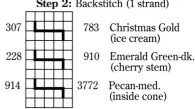